I0109963

COPING

KAREN PALLESGAARD MUNK

COPING

A Research Manual for Qualitative
Microanalysis of Stress Processes

AARHUS UNIVERSITY PRESS

COPING
A Research Manual for Qualitative
Microanalysis of Stress Processes
Karen Pallesgaard Munk

© The author and Aarhus University Press

Language revision: Mia Gaudern
Publishing editor: Lisette Agerbo Holm
Translator: Karen Pallesgaard Munk
Design: Carl-H.K. Zakrisson
Cover: Jørgen Sparre
Proofreading: Mark Eaton
Printer: Narayana Press, Denmark
Paper: Scandia Smooth Ivory
First edition: 2019

ISBN: 9788771849219

Published by:

Aarhus University Press
Finlandsgade 29
DK-8200 Aarhus N
Denmark
www.unipress.dk

International distributors:

Oxbow Books Ltd.
The Old Music Hall
106–108 Cowley Road
Oxford, OX4 1JE
United Kingdom
www.oxbowbooks.com

ISD
70 Enterprise Drive, Suite 2
Bristol, CT 06010
USA
www.isdistribution.com

This publication has been awarded a grant from
Aarhus University Research Foundation

MIX
Paper from
responsible sources
FSC
www.fsc.org
FSC® C010651

CONTENTS

1

2

3

4

5

6

PREFACE

This manual is meant for researchers carrying out qualitative explorations of negative or challenging events experienced by population groups or individuals. Its method offers a systematic and profound way of analysing processes related to existential burdens and their social, material and symbolic meaning to the individual. An important part of the analytical tool is the 'language' of emotions, which unfortunately tends to be excluded or simply overlooked in research. This does not seem so strange in quantitative research, which cannot account for subjectivity in the same way as qualitative research. A crucial part of subjectivity, however, is the subject's emotions, and their relation to his or her priorities in life – as well as both personal and cultural values. Emotions fluctuate throughout a person's life course, responding to progress towards (or indeed obstacles to achieving) their wishes and goals in life; this is also what we call *personal meaning*. The method is not concerned with the origins of these meanings, only with the fact that they constitute the orientation in life for the person in question and create *the* basis of stress and coping processes. The point is that the human being is a *prioritising* creature, which means that one thing is more important than everything else. If that were not the case, neither stress nor coping processes would take place. This fact is too often overlooked in stress research, and other kinds of research involving subjectivity for that matter. Qualitative methods are the most significant way of exploring this crucial part of subjectivity, because they are the only ones that make it possible to discover all the complex and contradictory facets at stake in existential burdens.

Although this book offers a method for exploring subjectivity and its relationship to perceived negative life events or episodes, it also stresses the importance of a parallel analysis of the objective conditions in which the individual is trying to cope with these events. In order to understand fully the individual's struggles, it is necessary to understand his or her cultural, social and material contexts as obstacles in life, sources of help or both. It should be emphasised that the notion of 'context' is broadly interpreted here: it also includes the physical body of the individual. The human ability to self-reflect and to see the bodily self as an object is important. The body (and mind) can be an opponent or a resource in life, depending on its health and capabilities.

It is very well known in the literature of coping and stress that individual coping processes rarely constitute the solutions to problems. Consequently, it is too narrow-minded to focus only on individual mental processes and actions, if we want to understand how stress and burdens are resolved – or not resolved – and also what their origins are. Here the notion of resources is an important analytic tool. It is an umbrella concept, which in principle can cover everything from a welfare society, money in the bank and emotional support from family and friends to good health. Behind this theme of the manual, furthermore, lies a philosophical and psychological idea of what a good life is, along with the recognition that we all struggle to realise even seemingly achievable – and sometimes less achievable – goals. Additionally, it should be stressed that the manual can be used anywhere in the world – in any culture. It is a premise of the analysis that emotionality, losses and threats in life are universal human dimensions. The personal and cultural differences can be found in *what* is important and *what* is vulnerable to challenges, threats and losses: that is to say, differences in personal and cultural *priorities*. Furthermore, variances can also be found in culturally specific ways of coping with these three categories of stress inducers.

This initial introduction to the analysis has highlighted the centrality of the concepts of *personal priority*, *context and resource* because they are linked to individual interpretations of challenges, threats and losses, as well as possible solutions.

The analysis is primarily built on the theory of the late American Professor of Psychology at Berkeley University, R.S. Lazarus, who dedicated his whole career to outlining a new psychological foundation for understanding stress from a transactional and emotional perspective. He became a pioneer in the field of stress and coping, and his theory is logical and scholarly. He effectively changed the whole field of psychology by introducing the perspective of stress. He engaged with the different traditions in psychology, including classical concepts in his theory and rejecting others as a result of very thorough argumentation as well as his own closely reasoned ideas. One of my colleagues at The Institute of Psychology at Aarhus University, Denmark, Professor Emeritus Eggert Petersen, referred to Lazarus as 'Mr Appraisal' because he addressed a shortcoming of the field in that stress research sometimes seems to forget completely this fundamental subjective dimension of human cognitive function: that we continually *appraise* the information coming to us in order to learn if it is or could be a threat, or imply a loss of something personally important. This is not always a conscious process, but a subliminal one that occurs beyond the level of selective consciousness, which is connected to more neutral activities in daily life. If something potentially threatening or actually threatening is happening, this subliminal process becomes conscious and demands the full attention of the individual. Behind the idea of subliminal monitoring lies an assertion that *control* over personally important affairs is crucial to human beings. I too think that Professor Lazarus deserves credit for raising the issue of this appraisal process, because it is needed in order to understand the initiation of a stress and coping process. While his theory cannot be characterised as a whole new psychology, making other traditions or perspectives superfluous,

I believe he laid a systematic and logic foundation for understanding human beings which is – at least to me – indispensable.

My contribution is to translate the theory of Lazarus into a qualitative tool and to develop his concept of 'emotional coping', which played only a minor part in the original theory. This is to some extent effected with the help of the above-mentioned Professor Emeritus Eggert Petersen's different dimensions of *resignation*.

However, the whole idea of 'translating' the theory into a qualitative tool has turned out to be a more fruitful one than I initially thought. Scientifically, it makes a huge difference whether the 'instrument' is restricted to quantitative measurements, for example in a rating scale, questionnaire, inventory, checklist, test, etc. Lazarus himself developed only quantitative tools (with Professor of Psychology, now emerita, Susan Folkman), primarily the famous WAYS ('Ways of coping questionnaire' – later revised), based on his theoretical work. In my opinion none of these quantitative tools had the ability to operationalise his very differentiated theory into a scientific tool that could help a researcher to dig deep down into the processes of the individual. In fact, I think that the WAYS takes the researcher in a direction that is directly opposite to the one the theory of Lazarus intended. In his work, Lazarus made an enormous effort to show how to avoid the personality trait 'dead-end' in stress research.[1] This is an analytical trap because it has the tendency to exclude completely the transactional, appraising, emotional, iterative and fluctuating aspects of the coping process that happens between the individual and their context in a broad sense.[2] This reveals that the WAYS is meant for *standardizing* coping processes into typical ways of acting during stress, without investigating *what* is at stake for the individual or the emotional reactions following the process – information that would help us understand the person, their situation, how they actually got the problem solved (if it was solved), and how the process perhaps contributed to development and changes in their situation.

Everything in WAYS is completely removed from its contexts and the specific situations of its informants. This is a significant shortcoming, and leads away from the differentiated and pioneering road of the theory of Lazarus. It is certainly unusual in the personality trait measurement tradition for a tool to be built on such a differentiated theoretical background; in the qualitiative tool of the extended version of the theory presented in this book, the advantages of this background are fully realised, avoiding the deficencies found in WAYS. This does not mean that I also do not recognise the existence of personality traits, but they do not figure in this book, where the analysis of the coping process is the aim. Professor Lazarus and others also saw the limitations of the WAYS, but did not manage to develop an alternative tool. In his last book, Lazarus (1999) has a chapter about narratives and emotions, but he did not include his whole theory of stress in the narrative perspective. One also has the impression when reading Lazarus that he was uncomfortable with methods other than quantitative research, in spite of him seeing its limitations. This story is just one instance of the typical conflict in scientific thinking between quantitative and qualitative methods, which also results in different conditions for publishing (Møller, Bengtsen & Munk, 2015).

Furthermore, I introduce the neo-Aristotelian philosopher Martha Nussbaum to Lazarus in the sections about emotions, as her work provides interesting philosophical additions to the theory. Nussbaum herself engaged with Lazarus in her book about emotions (2008).

I hope that researchers investigating all kinds of strain experienced by human beings will profit from the method presented here.

Aarhus 2019
Karen P. Munk

INTRODUCTION

This is a theory-driven analysis primarily built on the work of psychologist Richard S. Lazarus, with the addition of insights from philosopher Martha Nussbaum. This is necessary because Lazarus' notions of *goals* and *goal hierarchy* in my opinion tend to be overlooked by users of his theory; these concepts are in fact central to the theory, and very useful in investigating the reasoning of people who are in the middle of a coping process. Nussbaum's ideas are employed to emphasise this point that human beings are always struggling towards some kind of personal goal. These goals can also be defined as attachments to all kinds of objects – persons, ideologies, animals, dreams of the future, and so on – which is another way of expressing that human beings have ideas of 'the good life'. In the human sciences there are different theories of what this means more concretely. There is a long tradition, especially in philosophy and ethnology, of what the good life is in terms of means and ends (Aristotle, 2007 [384–322BC]; Damsholt, 2015). For Aristotle, the outcome is happiness. In this book there is a clear link to Lazarus' notion of the individual goal hierarchy, in spite of the fact that he is not specific about the means to the good life. In many respects, he depends on the universal characteristic of human beings being attached to self and surroundings, and posits that there is always a priority integrated into this phenomenon. Personal matters are the object of personal priority and meaning, wherever they come from. In the following analysis we are not concerned with where they come from – whether they are purely personal or culturally inherited – but only with their prioritisation by the person in question and thus their vulnerability to challenges, threats or losses, and, in turn, their relation to coping processes.

The premise is that people are struggling for the good life and some kind of happiness.

This critical notion of the individual goal hierarchy in the theory of Lazarus is often overlooked, and perhaps little understood, by the users of the theory. Stress only occurs when one has something important to lose; 'personal meaning' or personally important aspects of life are always at stake in a stress process. The philosopher Martha Nussbaum's work on emotions adds another dimension to this idea. Nussbaum herself refers to Lazarus in her book about emotions (Nussbaum, 2008). I do not know whether we could say Lazarus is a neo-Aristotelian, like Nussbaum – or perhaps call Martha Nussbaum a 'psychologist of emotions'. Both, however, share the same way of thinking about emotions. This conjunction will also underline the importance of analysing emotions as a helpful *tool* in understanding what exactly is at stake for a person experiencing stress.

Finally, it should be emphasised that this manual does not contain much theoretical discussion. However, it is essential to establish a basis for the analysis that explains the premises behind and the reasons for various aspects of the analysis. The first two chapters fulfil this purpose. The aim is to help the user of the manual to understand fully why the analysis is as it is – and not anything else. In order to undertake the kind of analysis detailed here the user must have grasped the arguments behind it. It would be a mistake to skip over these first two chapters; they are essential to conducting the microanalysis.

The first two chapters introduce the central terms and their development in Lazarus' theory. Nussbaum will be referenced in examinations of the notions of 'the good life', 'goal hierarchy' and emotions as an indication of personal values. Chapter Three is about the coping interview, and Chapter Four introduces the method of analysis. In the fifth chapter I introduce 'the life story of resources interview' – a special kind of interview that is deeply connected to the understanding of the present time and the resources at hand or not at hand to the person experiencing stress. If this last perspective is not relevant to your project, proceed to the sixth and last chapter, which is about how to present your results in publications.

THE CONTENT OF THE MANUAL

In the two introductory chapters the principal lines in the theory of Lazarus, including its development and supplements, are presented. Furthermore, a categorisation of the principal circumstances that may contribute positively and/or negatively to the course of individual coping will be offered. It was underscored in the Preface that the outcome of a coping course can rarely be explained by individual strategies alone. Therefore, a systematic overview of possible situations, from intentional to accidental interventions in the process, is provided.

In Chapter Two the focus is on change: what shapes the direction and content of the coping process? Particular attention is given to the kinds of interventions and life circumstances that influence the process in a positive and/or negative way for the coping subject. The coping process is dependent on the interpretations of the person and what he or she perceives is at stake, as well as on the social and material possibilities in their environment. Normally this will also be part of the appraisal process of the person: what are the realistic options for getting help? Here we have personal priorities meeting context/society and the 'hard facts of life' in a broad sense. In psychology, this is called the transactional perspective.

In Chapter Three the relevant aspects of the qualitative research interview are explained, and especially, of course, the coping interview. More specifically, the following aspects are addressed:

- the importance of a clear contract with the informants;
- the validity of memories of coping courses;
- lessons from the field of memory research; and
- the potential pitfalls of the research interview.

A guide to the coping interview is then presented.

Chapter Four is about the appraisal and coping analysis, and comprises an explanation of the concepts of the method and its procedure.

Chapter Five gives an example of a special life-history interview, called a 'resource interview', designed to investigate the 'luggage' of resources the informants of your coping research project bring with them. The focus in this type of interview is on transitions through the life course, because these are closely connected with the question of access to resources (Munk, 2012). This allows a deeper understanding of the informant and their options for coping with their situation.

In the last chapter suggestions are given for ways of presenting the results of the method in scientific articles. Finally, there is an Appendix that demonstrates the analysis in use, taken from one of my research projects.

CHAPTER 1

INTRODUCTION TO THE THEORETICAL BASIS OF THE RESEARCH MANUAL

Before presenting the theory, I will briefly explain the understanding of the notions of stress and coping used in the manual, since these concepts are used in very different ways both inside and outside the research literature.

THE CONCEPT OF STRESS

Many disciplines use the concept of stress in many different ways, because the theoretical and methodological contexts in which it is used diverge.[3] Typically, one of three distinctive positions is taken when attempting to understand stress:

1. *The perspective from inside and out*: Stress is connected with the ability of the person to endure strain; interpretations of inner life and social relationships are not relevant. Only personality traits are pertinent. The typical concept used here is 'resilience'.[4]
2. *The perspective from outside and in*: Stress is an influence related to certain life events, and as such also independent of interpretations of the person affected by the event. These situations are most often culturally prescribed as critical to the individual and consequently normative.[5]
3. *The relational perspective*: Stress occurs in a dynamic relationship between person and environment, as it is perceived and appraised by the person, but without neglecting the objective character of the situation.[6]

The last position is the foundation of this manual. It is concord-ant with contemporary psychology, which is moving away from dualistic models because they are insufficient in investigating the interpretive relationship of the subject to the environment. An ongoing transactional relationship between person and en-vironment (or, posed in a more philosophical way, *between subject and object*) is a foundation of modern psychology (Bron-fenbrenner, 1979; Bruner, 1958; Lazarus & Launier, 1978; Sameroff, 2009).[7] Historically there has been a tendency in the science of psychology either to consider individuals from a purely environmental perspective, free of the interpreting per-son, or to adopt a purely intra-psychic perspective, examining the individual independently of the influences of their environ-ment (Bronfenbrenner, 1979). This division refers to a classic conflict in psychology between different scientific ideals, which in turn stem from different understandings of what a human being is like. But it also refers to a – perhaps much deeper – theo-retical problem in philosophy and psychology about how to bridge the gap between the mental and the surrounding world, and to what extent the individual is influenced by their social and cultural context. This is a fundamental philosophical conflict in psychology.[8] The problem of how to find out what is going on in the inner world of the subject is another classical problem of psychology and other sciences of which the human being is the object. The first and second positions listed above represent the either–or dichotomy that neglects Thomas & Thomas' classic theorem (Bronfenbrenner, 1979: 23):

> If men define situations as real, they are real in their consequences.

The third position, the relational perspective, builds implicitly on this theorem, which recognises the transactional relationship between person and environment and the (deep) influence of perception and interpretation of the environment on cognition, emotions and behaviour. This is the mainstream position in modern psychology. It does not mean that the environment of the subject should be ignored in its objective sense (which is what happens when you only take a first-person perspective). The environment cannot be made to disappear through interpretations. The consequence is that every research project that studies a coping process should follow a double track: firstly, *the perspective of the subject on the environment – or the first-person perspective* on the environment, and secondly *the same environment* described as objectively as possible – independent of the subject under study. This perspective could also be called the 'life circumstances' of the person studied. This objectively described analysis is an *analysis of conditions*.[9]

The term 'stress', however, will be used very sparsely in the manual, precisely because the concept has obtained so many different meanings. Apart from the three mentioned positions, stress can also be 'positive' or 'negative', where 'positive' stress is related to constructive activity, and 'negative' stress is related to problems or burdens that do not disappear and are perceived as harmful by the person in question. Here, the terms 'burden' and 'negative emotions' will primarily be used. When the term 'stress' is used, it signifies only negative stress.

THE CONCEPT OF COPING

The term 'coping' has been used as an expression of a positive outcome in some theoretical traditions, but also in the language of daily life: 'He coped well with the situation?'; 'Can you cope?'. The psychodynamic tradition of 'coping with it' is generally opposed to pathology: 'coping' means solving problems, while non-coping or use of defences is considered a sign of pathology. Here, 'defence' is a concept from psychoanalysis, defined as an unconscious and pathological protection against anxiety. Lazarus does not use the concept in this way, however. The danger in using the term in the psychodynamic way is that judgement of a person's way of acting and reacting to a burden very easily becomes normative. The *personal meaning* of a situation is very easily overlooked, and it is personal meaning that decides whether a coping process is initiated. A dualistic and very categorical 'verdict' of 'normal'/'pathological' or 'right'/'wrong' could be the result. The transactional analysis in this book is not concerned with the categories of 'normal' and 'abnormal'. Rather, the objective is to investigate the particular perspective of the individual person in their struggle to regain control over important life issues. This does not mean, however, that we cannot analyse whether the person is acting appropriately in order to reach their goals. Are they really acting in accordance with their own interests?

In the psychodynamic understanding of the concept of coping we also find an underlying concept of control standing in for the 'normal', which is a debateable matter because the outset of a burden process is a loss of control and rarely does the person succeed in regaining control of the situation. This is seen, for example, in situations of irreversible losses. Situations of loss of control as part of the human condition could not by definition be called pathological. Sometimes – and very often – it is the social surroundings that intervene and solve the problems; sometimes they resolve themselves, as in the case of some diseases. In other words, we need a broader understanding of what is happening during the coping process when a person is struggling to regain control by attempting to mobilise resources that are not currently available to them. In the words of Lazarus, 'coping' is understood in the following way in this manual:

> Constantly changing cognitive and behavioural efforts
> to manage specific external and/or internal demands that
> are appraised as taxing or exceeding the resources of the
> person (Lazarus & Folkman, 1984: 141).

Lastly, a warning about the way coping processes are labelled in English: be aware of the terminology. Sometimes coping processes are called coping *strategies* or coping *mechanisms*. This last term must be considered a 'contradiction in terms', because coping processes, according to the understanding of Lazarus, are an expression of the person's *active and innovative* attempt to handle a difficult situation – in contradiction to the already learned and instinctive reactions built into the word 'mechanisms'.[10] Coping processes are never independent of the reflections of the person. On the contrary, a coping situation is – as mentioned earlier – by definition a new situation to the individual, which excludes a ready made answer to the situation. Therefore, the word *mechanisms* should not be used in connection with this understanding of coping.

A THEORY-DRIVEN RESEARCH METHOD

Coping microanalysis is a theory-driven method. This means that the theory constitutes a systematic frame for the investigation of coping processes, giving the researcher the opportunity to capture all kinds of variations connected with burdens and their expansion without falling into the normative trap about what is normal or pathological. In addition, it is often a problem in stress research that life events or situations are said to be 'traumatic or stressful' without analysing how these are interpreted by the person in question. Sometimes normatively stressful situations are not experienced as stressful.[11] The method presented here should give the researcher the opportunity to detect a complex and sometimes contradictory picture of how a person is interpreting their situation. A life event can develop in many different and unexpected ways, and the frame of analysis should be able to capture this.

The theory-driven method does not mean that you must know everything about an informant beforehand, or that you must split up the developing event into minor categories; on the contrary, it allows you to analyse a coping process fully, detecting new and unexpected complexities.

The method is both the theoretical framework of the analysis and a recipe of how it may be carried out in practice. Only the high-level concepts and definitions are offered, which point to the primary variations in meanings, emotions, actions and interventions, and finally suggest relevant parameters for evaluating the results of a coping process.

The following sections will treat the fundamental elements in the theory of Lazarus, taking a high-level view to introduce the key perspectives and concepts of the method. There is, by necessity, some repetition as the new concepts will be mentioned in different contexts: first when the concept of goal hierarchy is presented and second in the overview of the whole spectrum of coping acts of which the microanalysis is composed.

Lazarus attempted to solve a number of fundamental problems in psychology, regarding not only the person–environment relationship, but also the association between cognition and emotion: what comes first? Or: which is the cause of the other? As a consequence, Lazarus' work was relevant not just to stress research, but for psychology in general. It is important to understand, however, that his theory is *not* a general theory of action; it is a theory of stress that focuses on burdensome life events and the defensive positions subjects adopt in response to them. Normally when we talk about coping we are dealing with reactive more than proactive actions. People do also, however, develop proactive activities in order to prevent unwanted things happening when this is possible.

One of the strengths of Lazarus' theory is that he avoids the classical constraints that tend to prevent researchers from identifying what is really going on. These constraints are related to the aforementioned fundamental problems in psychology. They are:

- very simple explanations of personality traits, e.g. 'hardiness' or 'resilience';
- idealistic phenomenology which neglects the environment;

- behaviouristic approaches which neglect the subject;
- normative standards for coping processes and results (seen in psychoanalysis-inspired stress theories); and
- simple causal explanations of the relationship between emotion and cognition.

Ingeniously, Lazarus transcends the borders between different psychological traditions in a reflective and undogmatic attempt to solve some of these classical problems. There is good reason that Lazarus has become one of the world's most influential researchers of stress. At the same time, it is important to understand that he developed his theory over many years, and that new elements were always being added. These new elements primarily concerned emotions and their significance.

In Lazarus' theory, the human being is an active learning agent in their changing life circumstances. This fundamental unity of analysis was in place very early (Lazarus & Launier, 1978), but it does not mean – as pointed out earlier – that we are dealing with a general theory of action. Rather, the focus is that human beings struggle with burdens of many kinds, and these are always considered as relational problems. Stress is not isolated in either the subject or the environment, but precisely in the relationship between them (Lazarus & Folkman, 1984; Munk, 1999). A reaction of stress can only appear due to a combination of an event of some kind (in the environment, in the body or in the mind) *and* an interpreting subject with something that is emotionally at stake in the situation.[12] This vulnerable emotional engagement or attachment is fundamental; it is only these attachments that are the objects of coping processes. That is why it is crucial to the microanalysis to detect which attachments are under pressure or lost. The succeeding events will be directed by the type of event (its objective character) and the interpretation the subject makes of it. Detecting the personal meaning of a troubling situation is key to the method, and it is thus connected to a hermeneutic or interpretative tradition of science.

A CHANGE OF PERSPECTIVE

Originally Lazarus called his theory 'cognitive-phenomeno-logical'. Later on, he gave up this name in favour of 'cognitive-motivational-relational' (Lazarus, 1991). With this new name is underscored the active appraising and action-oriented perspective on the subject, as well as the contextual perspective – in contrast with 'cognitive-phenomenological', which could be misinterpreted as an understanding of the subject free of any context outside any dynamic relationship with their environments. The 'cognitive-motivational-relational' theory understands the subject in a narrow relationship to its environment, reads 'meaning' as relational meaning and views the relationship from a perspective of adaptation.[13]

The perspective of adaptation should not, however, be read as a traditional functionalistic perspective in which the individual is a passive, defensive, reacting creature giving in to the aims of other people and the contingencies of life, in spite of the fact that coping very often should be seen as exactly that. Instead, the adaptive perspective is a differentiated understanding of the human being and its life circumstances. Sometimes the subject is active and full of initiative, controlling and improving their circumstances, but sometimes and indeed often they have to resign themselves to adapting to conditions that cannot be changed. A typical example is a fatal disease for which there is no cure. Of course, people have different attitudes to the uncontrollable; however, death as a human condition is unavoidable. Another example could be politically determined life circumstances; political work can be seen as a kind of 'collective' coping, where a group of subjects strive together in order to change their shared life circumstances. Lazarus did not use the term 'collective' himself, but there is nothing in his theory that obstructs the use of this kind of coping perspective. In fact, it chimes well with a theory that takes a differentiated perspective on human beings and their life circumstances.

A SYSTEMIC ONSET

The fundamental fact of life that human beings are integrated into a biological, social and material environment has the consequence that you have to have a broad view on what contributes to instigating a process of coping – aside from personal judgements.

The consequence for Lazarus' theory is that it has its outset in a systematic, theoretical understanding, and the same goes for the kind of qualitative microanalysis presented in this book. This book is, however, more explicit about this than the theory of Lazarus.[14] It appreciates that at the onset of a coping process, its course and outcome is decided not by one or even a few matters, but – in principle – by the whole environment of the subject, as a 'partner' of the whole process.[15, 16] In this context 'environment' means all kinds of sources of influence outside the physical body of the person, 'nature' in a broad sense (i.e. the climate) and all levels in the social systems of which the subject is a part, including the systems of political states (Højrup, 2002).[17]

The body in some sense also belongs to the environment because we have the ability to reflect on ourselves and treat ourselves as an object, so to speak. When the body becomes ill, it is perceived as an object we cannot necessarily control. Here we are dealing with forces other than the power of the will. In that respect, our body is also 'nature' and can change the coping process in more or less unpredictable good or bad ways, as well, of course, as causing stress due to illness and therefore reduced capacity to function. The body is also a 'partner' in the creation of emotions, which are partly defined – by Lazarus and many others – by their physiological expressions.

The principle of systems also includes social systems comprising other people who have both common and individual agendas, and who are connected in states, societies, families and other sort of groupings with internal dependence and influences in sequences that are historical in nature (Dilthey, 1988

[1923]; Bronfenbrenner, 1979; Lazarus, 1991; Munk, 1999). The connection between the microanalysis and the systems to which the interviewed person belongs will be explained in the next section. Here it suffices to say that in order to understand the course of a mental strain a wide-ranging interpretation of the environment is essential to the analytic apparatus; coping courses are in no way directed solely by the actions or strategies of the person, in their outset or their outcome. A category called 'intervention' should always be included, covering all kinds of (disturbing) interferences and also (goal-oriented) initiatives that do not originate with the person themselves. To give a realistic picture of what helped or did not help in a situation of mental strain, this perspective is vital.

One could, perhaps, be tempted to see similarities between this theory and what in social-medical discourse is called a 'bio-psycho-social' perspective or a 'holistic' understanding. The difference is that the 'bio-psycho-social' approach represents an eclectic – ad hoc – mixture of many sorts of theories (science of nature, psychology and sociology) in order to explain many kinds of patterns of illnesses. Furthermore, in this social-medical discourse there is a tendency to view the subject as a passive victim of their life conditions (Wulff, Pedersen & Rosenberg, 1990). The systems theory of Lazarus is different: its focus is on the perceived burden on the active individual. It is a unified, consistent psychological theory.

THE GOAL HIERARCHY AS A LEADING PRINCIPLE

As mentioned above, a precondition of a stress reaction is a personally negative interpretation of a situation. Another precondition is the absence of adequate strategies to cope with the situation. This second fact will be explained more thoroughly later. In this section I will clarify the ideas about the human being that lie behind the theory of the initiation of a stress reaction.

Every human being has a personal attitude or key that is continually deciding what is good, bad or neutral in relation to their wellbeing. Lazarus called this key of personal values a *goal hierarchy*. This expresses the more or less stable and conscious attachment of a person to their environment – in a broad sense. Consequently, the person–environment relationship is always more or less emotional, and it is here that we find the background to the otherwise rather vague concept of 'personal meaning'. Attachments embrace not only concrete matters, such as the person themselves, other people, places and material objects; they also involve abstract matters such as ideas and symbolic values – including religions and political ideologies, which help shape our identities and give us a place in the world as persons. The consequence of this is that a perceived assault on something we believe in and use to orient ourselves becomes a threat to our very identity and person. This is why political and religious conflicts escalate, involving many more issues beyond what is immediately apparent.

While an individual's goal hierarchy is invisible, it has deep practical consequences, as it decides what is at stake in a situation of mental strain. Individual goals within the hierarchy are vulnerable and when threatened demand a kind of coping, for example the goal of maintaining good health is at stake if you receive a cancer diagnosis, or the goal of having a loved one around in your life is lost if they die. When it is the *priority* of goals in the hierarchy that decide the character and intensity of the mental strain, changing the goal hierarchy itself can also be a means of resolving the problem. The adjustment of goal priorities is thus also a coping strategy. In practice, this means that if your partner is leaving you, you could in principle choose to remove them from your goal hierarchy by telling yourself they were not worth caring about. The relationship with them is thus removed from your personal goal hierarchy, though of course this is not an easy thing to do.

THE CONCEPT OF GOAL – THE HEART OF THE THEORY AND METHOD

Lazarus defines a 'goal' in a fairly unusual way. The word normally expresses something that you consciously want to achieve, and Lazarus has been criticised for thus overemphasising the rational and conscious aspects of human endeavours. This is, however, a misunderstanding. It should be clear from his writings that his interpretation of the concept is quite the opposite. For Lazarus, a 'goal' can be any kind of emotional attachment – anything that is of value and importance to the subject. Such goals constitute the personal condition for the experience of threats and losses (stress), and the existential source of personal meaning in life. Furthermore, it is always one or more of those relational goals that is the object of healing or recovering activities in a process of coping. But why did Lazarus choose this term? It is obvious that the theory needed a label for personal priorities, and a choice had to be made. A closely related point of view is the Aristotelian theory that once their basic needs are satisfied in daily life, the goal of human beings is happiness (Aristotle, 2007 [384–322BC]). The question is: what brings you happiness? The 'good life' is, of course, different for different people and cultures, but as a human goal, it is thought to be universal. The personal idea of what the good life means to the individual is crucial in relation to burdens, distress and coping. During a person's life course their own definition may change, becoming integrated with their changing environments and developing an extended complex of symbols representing their goals.

Traditionally a 'goal' is both attractive and fundamentally motivating. The difference in the theory of Lazarus is that a 'goal' is not a project, rationally planned and laboriously achieved, or something that can be ticked off before proceeding on to the next goal. For Lazarus, attachments are only to some extent controllable and subject to our conscious and rational reflections.

Sometimes we do not even notice what is important to us before it is threatened or even taken away. It is our emotional reactions that tell us that something is wrong – this is why they are so useful as instruments of self-knowledge. A stressful situation always begins with the goal hierarchy of the subject, and goals are a 'sine qua non' of emotional reactions. Emotions are thus the key to understanding what is happening to the subject.

THE CONCEPT OF HIERARCHY

An important dimension of emotional attachments is priority, which is more or less unconscious. Threats to and losses of the top attachments in the hierarchy are more devastating than attachments at lower levels in the hierarchy. But our values are not rationally coordinated, and internal conflicts between values are possible (Nussbaum, 2004); painful emotional conflicts and dilemmas are common, due to unavoidable existential situations of choice (we find a good example of a dilemma in the case of the woman with a husband suffering from dementia used later in this book). The structure of the goal hierarchy, and its restructuring, are not conscious or rational, which is why we sometimes feel we are 'chosen' by our emotional attachments; we are not always masters of ourselves.[18] During a coping process, however, our attachments become clear to us and this allows us to relate rationally or consciously to the emotional engagements and actions that do not seem good, or in our own interest.

The goal hierarchy and consequently our ideas of the good life are built and rebuilt over our lives, in a transactional process with our personal development and environment. This means those things we want to control can change and new and important vulnerabilities can appear (an obvious example is having children).

THE GOAL HIERARCHY AND THE WELLBEING OF HUMAN BEINGS

The ability to construct a goal hierarchy of attachments is a precondition for the positive and negative emotional reactions that inform the individual that some things are more important than others. Furthermore, the individual struggles more or less consciously to realize the most important goals in the hierarchy and to obtain control over their life circumstances in order to make this possible. While ordinarily one might 'reach' a goal, here we say one 'realises' a goal, which means living in a happy, satisfying or at least to some extent harmonious relation with your main goals, that is, your idea of the good life. It is problematic, however, if the distance between one's goals/wishes/dreams of life and one's daily reality is too extreme. It is the goal hierarchy and its realisation that constitute the meaning of life for the individual, and it is this personal meaning of unhappiness or burdens we attempt to identify when we conduct a coping analysis. We cannot know beforehand what exactly is at stake for the coping person – even if the starting point of the analysis is some kind of life event, illness for example.

In his highlighting of the importance of the well-being of the subject in relation to stress and coping, Lazarus has always avoided relying on a principle of lust, which is seen primarily in psychoanalysis (Lazarus, 1991). It is obvious, however, that a notion or ontology of the human being as searching for happiness – besides many other things – and trying to eliminate discomfort is integrated into his theory and thereby also his method. The path to happiness and wellbeing can be very different between individuals and between cultures. Interestingly, however, even within Western cultures we have many more differentiated concepts of discomfort, unhappiness and negative emotions than of their positive equivalents. This could perhaps be seen as an expression of human fragility and vulnerability. Indeed, we have

no control at all over some of the most significant life circumstances: where we are born, and who our parents are.

THE ROLE OF THE GOAL HIERARCHY
IN THE COPING PROCESS

The impairment of an important personal goal is at the core of
the analysis. The goal hierarchy is thus essential for identifying
the target of the coping process. It bears repeating that the
impairment may be a result of something happening outside the
individual or of an act of the coping self ('I never imagined this
about myself'; 'I am disappointed in myself'; 'How could I have
done that?'; 'I regret that decision').

Understanding the goal hierarchy also helps us identify when
the position of goals in the hierarchy is itself an object of coping.
Goals can be removed from the hierarchy, moved to a lower
level or cease to be an object of realisation due to an irreversible
loss (i.e. the death of a loved one). The goal may lose its meaning
completely, or its emotional power reduced ('It is not as important as I thought in the first place'). In the manual this process is
called *extinction/reduction of values* and *active resignation*.[19]
Extinction of a value or goal means either its reprioritisation or
annihilation, and consequently the removal of the burden ('This
is not as important as I thought'; 'I have realised that it is not
worth this suffering'). Lazarus would probably have called this
a 're-evaluation', but I find it more precise to call it an 'extinction'.
A re-evaluation leads to the extinction of the value, for the
burden to be removed. It should be underscored, however, that
this is never a simple rational solution, and depending on one's
personality and the nature of the problem, may take many years.
Often it is not fully successful, resulting not in indifference but
in a bitterness that can be characterised as a kind of chronic anger.
The experience of deceit seems very often to have this consequence (Munk, 1999). Perhaps such anger or bitterness is caused

more by the loss of the attachment itself, or even the meaning it gave to the person's idea of the good life, more than by the loss of the object itself.

It is impossible to establish standards for these processes, but the crucial point is that in principle it is possible to remove a burden by eliminating a goal from the goal hierarchy. The goal hierarchy is both the basis of the theory and an 'instrument' in the coping process.

Another common obstruction to the realisation of our goals is the death of a loved one. While usually not intentional, it can be interpreted as a kind of 'deceit', thus provoking an emotional reaction of anger – as well as grief. But this does not mean that the love for the dead person is gone. In a certain respect, the goal is intact because it lives in one's memory. It cannot, however, be a part of a living transaction any longer. We therefore need a concept of coping that addresses the difference between wishes/dreams/disappeared attachments living in our memory and mind, and the possibility of realising them. This book refers to such a strategy as *active resignation*, which covers the process by which the person recognises their loss and even reinterprets it with a positive narrative and finds other (perhaps new) goals to live for. This change of attitude is also a way of making a burden disappear. The dreams or memories and emotional attachments are still there, but there is an acceptance that they will never be realised. This is why it is often said that new marriages in old age are very often a *trio* or a *quartet* of the new spouse, the widow(er) and the dead spouse(s). Acceptance is achieved by telling oneself that the awful loss was in essence a positive event. This is called the active resignative narrative, and it has three elements:

1. Acquittal: explaining why the loss happened and that the attached person is not to blame – in fact nobody is to be blamed;
2. Paradox: understanding that the alternative would have been worse, and so the loss was actually a blessing; and

3. After all: looking forward to the future by recognising that life is still good.

This is an anti-depressive narrative in the form of a consoling narrative of a grieving person. Later in the manual we will return to those forms of coping related to the goal hierarchy. An overview of the types of coping used in the method can be seen on p. 46.

The objective here is simply to point out that a coping process may also comprise an adjustment of one's goal hierarchy, and that there are two very different ways in which this can be done: *extinction of a goal* and *active resignation*. It is not correct to call these mental adjustments 'strategies', because they are not consciously planned acts. It is possible to plan to remove or loosen emotional ties and facilitate the process by certain activities, but you can never be sure that they will succeed. However, for practical reasons we use the term 'strategies' also for these adjustments.

These two 'strategies' fall into the category that Lazarus described as *emotion-focused* coping[20]. In an *extinction/reduction of values* the emotional attachment is removed or reduced, and in *active resignation* it is not affected. It should be mentioned that Lazarus also refers to a third type of emotion-based coping called 'palliative coping'. The only objective of this kind of coping is to calm the unpleasant emotions related to the situation, and *not* to remove the burden itself. This issue will be clarified later. It is not wrong to call these types of coping *emotion-focused*, but they are so various that it seems meaningless to put them into the same category. Instead I suggest a separation into three categories: *goal extinction, active resignation*, and *palliation*.

EMOTIONS AS A 'SECOND LANGUAGE'

Towards the end of his career Lazarus developed his theory to include emotions.[21] This made emotions an important tool of interpretation in the method, as their often contradictory complexities help reveal the many perspectives that together make up the personal meanings attached to burdens or life events. It is also the case that these personal meanings can help to explain puzzling contrasts in emotions – for example, when they are related to different, and perhaps incoherent, meanings.

In Lazarus' theory, 'thinking and emotion' are viewed as integrated but distinct aspects of mental life; they represent diverse channels of information. The emotions tell the person indirectly, with his or her whole body, about the actual state of the transaction with the environment (Lazarus, 1991; Nussbaum, 2004).[22] Thinking, on the other hand, is a conscious and purposeful activity connected to the practice of daily life. The 'cognitive' content of emotions is made up of unique or distinct narratives about what is at stake in ongoing transactions, and whether those transactions produce a positive or negative effect. These distinct narratives are called 'core relational themes' in the terminology of Lazarus. They tell a person something about a concrete relationship, and always involve a statement (threat to, loss of or gain for) about one's ego-identity.[23] If you are jealous, you feel a threat to an important relationship: for instance, a child may be jealous of a sibling who seems to occupy more of their parents' attention. This is an interpretation of a threat of loss of the parents' love. If you are envious, you want something that someone else has and that you consider valuable. Both examples include a threat to the ego-identity of the person and comprise a narrative of something not being right in a relationship from the subject's point of view. These themes will be explained more thoroughly in the chapter about method.

At this point it is necessary to clarify the difference between 'emotional attachments' and 'emotional reactions'. Briefly, these are two distinct, but similar, dimensions of a person's emotional life. 'Emotional attachments' testify to the human ability to make personally significant and committed relationships that exist over time and across contexts, and can develop throughout one's life course – thus constituting the personal goal hierarchy.

The dimension of 'emotional reactions', on the other hand has been precisely defined by the Danish neuropsychologist Anders Gade, following Lazarus:

> Emotions are deviances from the normal state, often in a rather short-term way – from seconds to hours in our experience, but usually only seconds in their bodily expression. Normally they deviate from simple feelings of desire or distaste by being aroused by what we experience or remember more than only by a stimulation of the senses. They deviate from sensations of the body and mood by breaking out in a situation which always comprises the surroundings (or a memory about it). They are more short-lived and usually also more intense than moods, and they usually have an object. Normally we do not get afraid, but afraid of something particular. On the other hand, temperaments are traits which characterize the personality. (…) An important dimension of emotions are that they are co-deciding what we are thinking of, and that they change our inclination or readiness to act. Emotions often make us change how we prioritize our different activities and in this way, they are the most important incentive behind our actions. (…) Emotions have three components: physiological arousal, motor activity and the subjective experience (Gade, 1997: 342, my translation).

Gade also points out that memories are able to awaken forgotten emotions, which is relevant to the coping interview and the validity of coping memories, addressed in Chapter 4.

To add to this picture, Nussbaum (2004) argues that emotions should not be seen as a kind of thoughtless, natural energy without any connection to the world:[24]

> What, then makes the emotions in my example unlike the thoughtless natural energies I have described? First of all, they are about something: they have an object. My fear,

my hope, my ultimate grief, they all are about my mother and directed at her and her life. A wind may hit against something, a current may pound against something, but these are not about the things they strike in their way. My fear's very identity as fear depends on its having an object: take that away and it becomes a mere trembling or heart-leaping. In the same way, the identity of the wind as wind does not depend on the particular object against which it may pound.

Second, the object is an intentional object: that is, it figures in the emotion as it is seen or interpreted by the person whose emotion it is. Emotions are not about their objects merely in the sense of being pointed at them and let go, the way an arrow is let go against its target. Their aboutness is more internal and embodies a way of seeing. It is to be stressed that this aboutness is part of the identity of the emotions. What distinguishes fear from hope, fear from grief, love from hate – is not so much the identity of the object which might not change, but the way the object is perceived: in fear, as a threat, but with some chance for escape; in hope, as in some uncertainty, but with a chance for a good outcome; in grief as lost; in love as invested with a special sort of radiance. Again, the adversary's view is unable to account for the ways in which we actually identify and individuate emotions, and for a prominent feature of our experience of them.

Third: these emotions embody not simply ways of seeing an object, but beliefs – often very complex – about the object. It is not always easy, or even desirable, to distinguish between an instance of *seeing x as y*, such as I have described above, from the belief that *x is y*. In order to have fear – as Aristotle already saw it – I must believe that bad events are impending; that they are not trivially, but seriously bad; that I am not in a position to ward them off;

that, on the other hand, my doom is not sealed, but there is still some uncertainty about what may befall. In order to have anger, I must have an even more complex set of beliefs: that there has been some damage to me or to something or someone close to me; that the damage is not trivial but significant; that it was done by someone; that it was done willingly; that it would be right for the perpretrator of the damage to be punished. It is plausible to assume that each element of this set of beliefs is necessary in order for anger to be present: if I should discover that not x but y had done the damage, or that it was not done willingly, or that it was not serious, we could expect my anger to modify itself accordingly or recede. ……….. Only an inspection of the thoughts will help discriminate. Here again, then, the adversary's view is too simplistic: severing emotion from belief, it severs emotion from what is not only a necessary condition of itself, but part of its very identity.

Finally: there is something marked in the intentional perceptions and the beliefs characteristic of the emotions: they are all concerned with value, they see their object as invested with value. The value perceived in an object appears to be of a particular sort – although here I must be more tentative since I am approaching an issue that is my central preoccupation. The object of the emotion is seen as important for some role it plays in the person's own life. The emotions are in a sense localized. The emotions appear to be eudemonistic – that is, concerned with the agent's flourishing (a system of ethics that bases moral value on the likelihood that good actions will produce happiness). In a eudemonistic ethical theory, the central question asked by a person is 'How should I live?' The answer lies in the person's conception of eudaimonia, or human flourishing (Nussbaum 2004: 187-189).

THE THREE-PART STRUCTURE OF THE COPING PROCESS

The trigger

It is a fundamental hypothesis in the theory of Lazarus[25] that human beings try as much as possible to control their most important life circumstances – this is done by, among other things, more or less unconsciously and instinctively monitoring and evaluating impressions in order to detect any threats to one's life or wellbeing (Lazarus, 1991; Carpenter, 1992). Lazarus calls this the 'appraisal process'. Subconscious monitoring was also considered a fact earlier on, by the Russian neuropsychologist Luria (1983), who believed it had a biological origin. According to Lazarus the process consists of a primary and then a secondary stage. During the *primary stage* the person is more or less subconsciously judging the situation and whether it seems likely to develop into a burden that could mean a threat to or a loss of a goal from the personal goal hierarchy. *The secondary stage* is an investigation of the resources available to prevent or even eliminate the threat (Lazarus & Folkman, 1984).[26] If a threat or a potential loss looms and there are no preventative sources available, then *coping courses* begin, which could be called the *third stage* in the process. But to emphasise: a perceived threat or loss related to the personal goal hierarchy is a necessary and sufficient condition for provoking a coping process. The process can last until the situation is resolved in one way or another, or not resolved at all. As we all know, problems do not always disappear but can become chronic – a neverending *third stage*. The principal question here is whether we can talk about a continual or long-lasting coping course when there is a problem that will not disappear. The answer is yes – because there is still a burden and reduced wellbeing to address. There are different possible trajectories in this situation:

- The person may give up, trying only to reduce the discomfort and unpleasant emotions following the situation. Here this is called 'palliative coping'.
- The person may continually try to solve their problems and use palliative coping at the same time.

It is important, however, to understand that a coping course is not necessarily limited in time. Neglecting this fact would mean overlooking the defensive and undesirable patterns of life that can follow a lifelong handicap.[27] When a problem is solved or your research project ends, you could also talk about a *fourth stage*: the outcome of the process, or whether the problems were solved or not.

It is now worth investigating the stages of the appraisal process in more detail.

Stage one:

The first part of the appraisal process results in one of three different conclusions about the relationship between the situation and the personal goal hierarchy (or attachments). The situation can be:

1. *Irrelevant* to the wellbeing of the person, meaning no emotional reactions and no need to initiate coping processes.
2. *Relevant* and *benign*, because the situation is a help to realising the goal(s) of the person. This is also called *goal congruence*. The result is positive emotional reactions and no coping.
3. *Relevant* and *malignant*, because the situation is appraised as a threat to the goal(s) of the person if there are no coping options. This is also called *goal incongruence*. It provokes negative emotional reactions and coping.

Furthermore, the third conclusion is divided into the following three (appraisal) categories:

- *Threat*: the possibility of a future loss;
- *Loss/damage*: irreversible or time-limited loss; and
- *Challenge*: a perceived potential gain or loss.

The last category, challenge, is ambiguous: it comprises the potential for loss as well as for reward. If the person tries, and the loss is avoided, he or she will profit in some way or another. If the person does not succeed with their struggle, or does not actively meet the challenge, the result can be some kind of loss.[28] A typical example is exams; another is sports competitions. Which of the three categories the relevant and malignant event belongs to depends on the person's options for preventing a negative outcome.

Furthermore, it is important to realise that the same event has the potential to cause many kinds of goal incongruences, or indeed a mixture of congruence and incongruence at the same time. If an event has a certain level of complexity, it will encompass a multiplicity of meanings to the person, for example the same event may be a gain in some ways and a loss in others. It is crucial for the researcher to catch these contradictions.

To illustrate this complexity, we can analyse a case of a death of a spouse suffering from dementia.[29] This event can be both a loss and a gain: a loss because the spouse is loved, and a gain because the feelings for the person were affected by the difficulties of caring for a beloved, but demented person. It is a relief, then, to be freed from the obligation of care. In this case it can be a social trap to appear as happy as you actually are, because this violates social norms about how to react to the death of a person; you can lose social recognition if you seem too happy. Furthermore, the loss can also occur in your own self-respect, as you may find it immoral in yourself to be happy about a death (a case similar to this is further elaborated in the appendix. The difference between the two cases is that the case in the appendix is about a spouse who was not loved by his wife and carer).

Stage two:

When the result of the appraisal process is that the situation appears to embrace some kind of goal incongruence (*relevant* and *malignant*), the logical next step is to start a search for the means to prevent the worst happening. The last necessary condition for initiating a coping process is that the person cannot find any means or has no strategies either to stop the malignant situation causing irreversible losses or to delay it (in which case they return to stage one at some late stage).

It should be mentioned that the step-by-step appraisal process described by Lazarus is not used in this manual. The focus here is on the conclusion of stage one and two in combination, concentrating on instances where there is goal incongruence (a threat or a loss), as well as defining the goal and its personal meaning more concretely. The reason for this is that the individual's final categorisation of an event is based on both stage one and stage two – nothing can be concluded before we know whether any kind of help is available.

Finally, it should also be mentioned that Lazarus (1991) differentiates between the intensities of situations of goal congruence and goal incongruence: how good or bad is it? He operates with six types of ego involvement, which indicate how intensely the person experiences the gain or threat against their wellbeing. These are his six issues connected with ego identity ('Who am I?'):

1. Self-worth and social recognition
2. Moral values
3. Ego ideals
4. Ideas and opinions
5. Other people and their wellbeing
6. Goals in life

A greater number of types of ego-involvement in a relevant and malignant situation reinforces the stress reaction. According to this author, however, one or more of the six types are *always* implicated in a situation of mental strain, and as mentioned earlier all six issues are part of the goal hierarchy. They are mentioned here to underscore the importance of always having an eye on those more or less intangible aspects of a stressful situation, since they can constitute independent motives. Sometimes – and more often than you might think – they are the *only* causes of mental strain. Threats to our wellbeing are not necessarily threats to concrete, material life circumstances – they could threaten our worlds of symbols and self-identities. These subtler issues show how difficult it can be to register and then understand what is going on in a given situation (see the example in chapter three).

Table 1. The course towards a coping process

1. Something happens in the environment – whether accidental, or caused by the subject or other people.

2. The subject carries out an appraisal process, the result of which may be: a. the event is *irrelevant* to their wellbeing; b. the event is *congruent* with their goal hierarchy; or c. the event is *incongruent* with their goal hierarchy.

3. The subject determines there is a goal incongruence: the event is appraised as a threat or loss due to the absence of means of reducing or removing it, or the event is appraised as a challenge with potentialities for loss or triumph.

4. Negative emotional implications are felt.

5. A coping process begins.

DIFFERENT TYPES OF COPING

As mentioned in the section *The goal hierarchy as leading principle*, this manual has its own way of differentiating coping strategies. In this section the whole range of coping categories used in the microanalysis will be explained. This also means there will be some repetition, which will hopefully also help to clarify how the system of analysis is built. In Table 2 below you will see a comparison between Lazarus' system and that of the micro-analysis.

At the outset we need to accept that a definitive coping analysis must be built on a system of all possible types of coping strategies, not least because it is the foundation for comparing research. The method is built on the following principles:

- The strategies are defined in the context of their aims regarding the personal meanings of the subject and NOT as acts visible to the environment. One can never know exactly the purpose of the performing subject; the same act may have several purposes at the same time. In the analysis you look for the motive or motives – that is the personal meanings – behind the visible act.[30]
- The strategies are mutual exclusive,[31] and cover on an abstract level the whole spectrum of possible strategies that can be found anywhere in empirical research on processes of coping.

As mentioned earlier, Lazarus created two problematic, but attractive main categories of coping strategies, apparently differentiated by their aims: *problem-focused* and *emotion-focused* coping.

According to Lazarus, *problem-focused* coping is outward action to resolve problems. In a way this is sufficient. However, using this category you can easily overlook the fact that problem-focused coping comprises two possibilities: 'prevention' of irreversible conditions (before they happen) and 'cure' or delayed solutions in the case of reversible conditions (which have occurred, i.e. a broken leg). It thus seems more correct or precise to differentiate between preventive and restorative problem-solving or coping, because losses can be momentary. The labels 'preventive' and 'curing' coping can also be applied to the aforementioned category of 'collective coping', concerning political work, which aims to be both preventive and problem-solving.

Emotion-focused coping is, on the other hand, a bit of a messy category because it covers various types of strategies with different objectives. They are all focused, however, on strategies that are introverted and aim to relieve or change the person's emotional state. However, their aims in relation to the problem are fundamentally different. This is especially true for the strategies of *resignation* and *emotional palliation*. If these strategies are confused, the result is a confused analysis, because *resignation* is a strategy that also resolves personal problems – admittedly in a special way, but this does not go for *palliation*. *Resignation* means giving up an active realisation of an emotional engagement, in the language of Lazarus a 'goal' in the personal goal hierarchy, but this does not entail an abandonment of the goal as of personal value. The love for the lost goal is intact, even if it is no longer possible to realise an active relation with it. Active resignation, however, does allow the subject to revive a 'normal' everyday life, and in this respect, it can be said that the strategy removes the problem. It should be emphasised that the process of active resignation is mostly slow and connected with grief, which never really disappears, but changes character during the process.[32] Palliation of emotions, however, does not aim in itself to dissolve the problem, but only to reduce the unpleasant emotions it provokes. Of course, this can be a help in problem-solving, but it is common when palliative strategies are used for them to become the only kind of strategies in a coping situation. This can evolve into quite an unhealthy life pattern, attempting to ignore unsolved problems and even creating new ones in what becomes a vicious circle.

Another weakness of Lazarus' categorisation is that it lacks a third, and necessary, category, which I call *goal extinction*. The aim of this strategy is to eliminate a goal from the personal hierarchy. Logically reprioritising or removing threatened goals can also resolve the problem. For the system of categorisation to be complete, there must be room for this third strategy.

Finally, we also encounter cases where a person does nothing at all to act on their personal problems – neither externally nor internally. This means that we must also account for passivity in our system. In the microanalysis this is called *passive resignation* (Petersen, 1985).[33] As a way of measuring the adequacy of this categorisation of strategies, various narratives expressing each category will be investigated in what follows. It is important to remember here that in very complex situations of mental strain it is possible to find the whole spectrum of different strategies activated more or less in relation to the whole complex of different personal meanings connected to the situation.

One last category of coping strategy covers the possibility of environmental intervention – in a broad sense.[34] The outcome of problematic situations very often cannot be explained with personal strategies (Pearlin, 1991; Munk, 1999). One must also look at the environment of the subject: was there help available or only conditions that made things worse – or was the problem entirely personal? Usually, 'intervention' refers to conscious and more or less goal-oriented acts by human beings. But interventions may also be made by nature in a broad sense – for example, in the natural healing of diseases, independent of the coping person and independent of their initiatives. If the coping subject intervenes (for example by asking for help), this should not be called 'intervention' but 'coping'. It should also be emphasised that interventions are not necessarily positive. They may also be negative, making things worse for the person in question. Very often relatives are considered a resource in gerontology, but they can also be the opposite, for example when adult children exploit their ageing parents. Other interventions are made by conditions in society, for example an economic crisis makes it more difficult to sell a house, which is crucial in a situation of divorce (read the constructed but realistic case in Chapter 3). Table 2 compares the terms of Lazarus and the microanalysis.

Table 2. Comparison of terms in Lazarus and the microanalysis

| Source of initiative | Coping strategies | | Aims in relation to the threatened or suffering goal |
	The microanalysis	Lazarus	
The coping subject	1. Preventive	Problem-focused	Maintenance of status quo
	2. Restoring problem solving		
The coping subject	3. Active resignation	Emotion-focused	Permanent change of status quo: giving up the realising of a goal in the goal hierarchy
The coping subject	4. Goal extinction	–	Permanent change of status quo: removal of a goal from the goal hierarchy
The coping subject	5. Palliation	Emotion-focused	No solution or change of status quo: only emotional relief
(No initiative at all)	6. Passive resignation	–	No solution or change
The environment	7. Intervention	–	Possible improvement or worsening of the situation

OUTCOME OF THE COPING PROCESS

Normally, analyses of coping do not include information on whether a permanent change resulted from the process. It must, however, be of a certain interest to research to find out how the process ended. Coping processes sometimes result in mental changes, for example a more differentiated experience of the self and the environment. This should be called 'development'. On the other hand, the mental outcome may be the opposite: more rigidity, a narrowed perception of the self and the environment and even mental illnesses such as depression. When this information is included in a coping analysis, it allows for the instigation of the developmental potential of the subject. The transitions – such as shifting roles – in life with which burdens are most often connected are also opportunities for development, by gaining a more differentiated view of the self and learning about one's social systems or environment (Bronfenbrenner, 1979). In most benign situations this can also entail improved ability to act appropriately for the good of the self and others. This aspect of a coping course is seen most explicitly in the interview, as well as in the analysis, when the coping process has finished – or when one's research project is over, which is not always the same thing. In final reflections, one often recognises that changes have taken place – whether major or minor.

SUMMARY

Stress reactions do not arise without the input of an environment and an interpretation of the environment, and this interpretation builds on the crucial and stable engagements that constitute the goal hierarchy of the subject. It is the relationship with the environment that suffers, and it is this relationship that is the object of a coping process. Depending on what is wrong, the result may be the restoration of the relationship or a permanent change in the relationship. The microanalysis operates with seven different types of coping strategy, as opposed to Lazarus' two. These seven types cover all kinds of coping courses. In the analysis we also explicitly operate with a broad concept of environment (including social systems, persons, nature, the subject's body and accidents). In the final conclusion, the outcome of the coping course is investigated in terms of developmental and other changes in the life of the subject.

CHAPTER 2

THE FORMATIVE ELEMENTS OF THE COPING COURSE

In the first chapter, the theoretical background to the analytical framework presented in this manual was introduced, in order to give an overview of the various factors involved. Among other things the concept of *resource,* in a broad sense, plays a prominent role in a coping context.[35] Threats to health, personal finance, life circumstances and so on all express vulnerability, which can be seen as an absence of resources. Most people will be exposed to some kind of shock or setback in their lives; statistics, research reports and basic common sense all suggest, however, that well-off and well-educated people live longer and better lives than people who are less privileged and less educated (see Lynch et al., 2000; Deaton, 2003; Due et al., 2003; Holstein et al., 2009). This is very likely due to differences in economic/material, intellectual, cultural and social resources, which – when accessible – contribute to preventing or repairing the consequences of setbacks in life. For instance, well-educated, wealthy people are less exposed to poor working environments, which have a negative influence on both mental and physical health.

People living in societies with a certain level of mutual solidarity are also less vulnerable, as social and economic support can contribute to coping courses. In my own research on coping among well-functioning older adults, 50% of coping courses were resolved with help from the welfare state and from their own informal networks (Munk, 1999). It was obvious that many of the problems my participants experienced could never have been solved solely by their own strategies and/or individual resources. The most obvious examples were access to free medical help and hospital treatment, home help and rooms for relatives at nursing homes for people suffering from dementia – not to mention pensions and other types of economic support, such as subsidies for housing. This kind of help alone reduces the worst kind of poverty among older adults.

Six aspects of a situation of mental strain seem to be crucial to the direction of a coping course:

1. The objective character of the situation;
2. The subjective character of the situation;
3. The level of perceived reversibility;
4. Emotional implications;
5. Personal resources; and
6. Social and environmental resources.

1. THE OBJECTIVE CHARACTER OF A SITUATION OF MENTAL STRAIN

By this is meant the initiating occurrence as it appears independently of the perception of the individual; that is, without the personal perspective of relevance. The objective character of the situation – which could be chronic illness, or perhaps temporary unemployment – sometimes sets up forceful restrictions on what can be done in order to restore the person's idea of balance in life. This objective perspective could be compared to looking up the symptoms of a disease in a medical textbook, where they are described independently of the person whose body is experiencing it. This description does not include the personal consequences the disease might have for a concrete person. In the analysis the terms for this objective aspect could be, for example: 'disease and death of a close relative', 'own disease', 'divorce', 'existential problems of close relatives', 'sentence for criminal acts', 'conflicts at work or in the family', 'natural disaster', 'changes in society' (the type of change should be specified) or 'retirement due to old age or illness'. In other words: the events are observed externally and formally, and consequently described without any personal implications.

It might be banal to point out that no coping course takes place in a vacuum: it has its outset and determination from problematic biological, material and/or social conditions in the environment, including the body of the person. In everyday language we might call these 'the hard realities of life', since more or less every human being is destined to experience conditions that fall into certain environmental categories and can be described in general terms. As mentioned earlier, the specific symptomatology of an ailment to be found in a medical textbook will play a role in the coping course of a person suffering from it. But there is quite a difference between a broken shoulder, a cordial thrombosis and a cancer in the bladder. These different objective, illness-related situations are profoundly different from social circumstances, such as stigma surrounding people accused of sex crimes, or the existential problems of close relatives, as seen in situations of unemployment. This is related to structures in society (economy, production, conditions on the labour market, the law, methods of government and normative directions), which are also objective realities to the person under mental strain, and should therefore be described by the researcher. The same goes for death, which has the objective consequence that the dead person leaves an empty space in the social system, and no matter how skilfully other members of that system cope, it is not possible to change this hard fact. When you come to think of it there are – sadly – many conditions that we cannot control.

There is, however, one type of event that is a bit tricky here, namely tense social relationships or direct social conflicts, which cannot be described without the subjective perspectives of the people involved; it is the collision of or difference between people's perspective or interests that objectively defines the situation.

Finally, it is important to pay attention to the fact that several types of objectively different events can happen to the same person at the same time, or successively in a course of incidents. These can interfere with one and another in a complex and often reinforcing way. For example, an illness may mean a person cannot work, which objectively gives them very different issues to cope with. It is obvious that the objective traits of distressing events contribute considerably to variation in coping courses, and to the outcome of coping processes. This also means that it makes no sense to talk about coping strategies in an abstract way without knowing the concrete situations behind them.

Mental illnesses and the objective character of a situation

The purpose of this manual is to aid research about ways of coping among all kinds of people from all kinds of groups. It is a premise, however, that our informants have a kind of rational insight into their problems and are able to be objective about their difficulties to some extent, too. In cases of physical illness, we try to understand the illness in the abstract. But this is not necessarily the case when we are dealing with people suffering from mental illnesses, which are connected with disturbances of self-perception. As a result, the category of objective traits of a situation should also include the subject's level of self-perception.

In cases of mental illness, it can be decisive to compare the person's interpretation with what is actually happening; the interpretation of self and environment can often be unreliable, due to the influence of the illness.[36] For example, in some types of depression there is no direct causal relationship between external events and the emotional state of the person and their ability to act. It can be difficult to understand what the problem is when the objective analysis of the situation draws a blank.[37]

An important exception is found in the diagnosis of geriatric depression, often the result of an accumulation of traumatic life events such as loss of a spouse, illness, economic problems and so on. In the international research literature there is agreement that this type of depression is related to poor quality of life in old age and has nothing to do with genetic disposition to depression (Munk, 2007). It is always true, however, that depression – no matter the cause – is not a type of suffering the subject can cope with directly, as they might with a physical illness. On the contrary, they lose the ability to reflect and to act as a consequence of the state of depression itself. This means that it is more meaningful to talk about *how you cope when you have a depression*, than *how you cope with a depression*, the latter unfortunately being a typical way of expressing the connection between coping and depression. It is very important to understand the difference.

It is similarly complicated to analyse people with psychoses that do not originate with depression.[38] Psychotic delusions and hallucinations also result in a twisted perception of the whole or parts of objective reality. It can consequently be very difficult to understand the acts of a person suffering from psychoses, not least because what they believe they have to cope with is not always clear. But there is an internal logic between the acts of a psychotic person and their interpretation of the situation; the ability to act in continuation of the personal interpretation of the situation is usually intact (Bender, 1998), and it is the distorted perception that governs the ensuing coping course. This is a complicated situation to analyse, because a mentally ill person can of course have other kinds of objective problems to cope with too, which have nothing to do with the mental illness. However, mental illness does often create social and material problems in itself.

The conclusion here is that a researcher should investigate the objective character of a situation of mental strain, independent of the perception and interpretation of the subject. At the same time, they should realise that the objective situation is a necessary but not a sufficient condition to create mental strain.

The personal interpretation of the sufferer is needed too. This will be treated in the next section. Finally, in the wake of objective events very often follows a role transition or change in social position for the person in question – for example, to patient, unemployed person or convicted criminal. These role transitions, which are also constituted by the person's social system, can also be seen as objective events.

Summary

While this manual takes pains to insist that it is the personal meaning or subjective perspective of events that provoke stress and coping courses, the objective character of events – understood as the social, biological and material realities with which the subject interacts – is an unavoidable co-player in a coping course. This is because 'hard reality' limits the opportunities people have to restore their situation to the status quo. Mental illnesses form a special case here, since sufferers' distorted perceptions of reality can make it difficult to analyse the relationship between objective events and personal interpretations.

2. THE SUBJECTIVE CHARACTER OF A SITUATION OF MENTAL STRAIN

This perspective could also be said to focus on the *interior of the mental strain*, that is, the subject's personal perspective on their situation, which we have already defined as the experience of a loss or a threat to personal goals. This is the part where we pinpoint what is converting the situation into one of mental strain for the person. The objective event has traits that make it both relevant and also incongruent to the goal hierarchy of the subject (as shown in Table 1). Finally – as stressed earlier – there are no resources perceived to be available to help the subject deal with the situation.

This is a repetition and affirmation of the concepts of primary and secondary appraisal from the theory of Lazarus (Lazarus, 1991). It is striking, however, how coping acts are *only* directed towards subjective traits of events and *nothing else*.[39] Furthermore, it is also striking, but obvious, that those personal perspectives have their roots in the life history of the person and also in their current social and material situation. In this way the same situation, such as caring for a spouse with dementia, can affect two people in very different ways. Did the couple have a loving relationship, did they work together or otherwise have a mutual material dependency before the onset of the dementia? Where the relationship was one of deep affection, more patience will be extended to the spouse suffering from dementia and more grief will be experienced when they die. On the other hand, a person in a less loving marriage may be less patient and even experience feelings of happiness and relief after the death of their spouse, which may cause trouble with feelings of guilt and shame (Munk, 1999; Haaning, 2000). These two cases are obviously distinct. Accumulated bitterness in a marriage may also play a role; the new vulnerability of the demented person can provoke their spouse to take revenge on them for years of perceived suppression. This almost seems to be a psychological regularity when the balance of power in a resentful couple changes, so that the formerly dominant person becomes weak.

In spite of differences in life historical backgrounds, objectively similar life events will in many ways frame a similar situation for the coping course. The cases will probably have some aspects in common, while others will be markedly different. You will not know beforehand how the situation has been appraised by the subject, and so you must be careful not to be prejudiced – especially if the case is about violating norms, such as being relieved and happy about the death of a relative. What can look like a loss from the outside can actually turn out to be a perceived gain in the subject's perspective.

Summary

It is the personal perception or appraisal that decides whether a situation becomes a burden, and in what manner. This personal perspective is crucial in order to identify exactly what the aim of the coping process is. This fact contributes to individual variation, because the same type of event may be a burden to some people but not others due to differences in goal relevance and goal congruence, which stem from different life histories. But even in cases of goal relevance and goal incongruence among people who have very similar life experiences, very often different kinds of appraisals will decide which *aspects* of the event give it negative or positive goal relevance. It is this subjective appraisal that a researcher should understand without prejudice, because it is decisive for the coping course, in combination with objective conditions.

3. THE LEVEL OF PERCEIVED REVERSIBILITY OF THE BURDEN

Whether the person under mental strain thinks that something can be done to remedy the situation or not deeply affects the ensuing coping course. The situation may be perceived as *irreversible*; the opposite possibility is *perceived reversibility*. There are in fact three possibilities when it comes to levels of reversibility:

- *Perceived irreversibility* is seen in cases of irreparable losses. The subject will not take any initiative to try to restore the loss, because it is perceived as impossible. If the burden will then disappear, a mental adaptation is needed; active resignation or extinction of the goal from the goal hierarchy are the only possibilities for overcoming the loss.

- *Perceived reversibility* is connected with the perception of a threat or a time-limited loss. In principle it should be possible to solve such problems, and the subject will therefore try to regain the status quo.
- *Perceived ignorance of reversibility* occurs when the foundation for any decision is objectively unknown, and choices of actions thus rest on faith or ideas of probability.

The last possibility, *perceived ignorance of reversibility*, is in a certain respect the most troublesome and at the same time a very common situation: one cannot know what the outcome might be of a cancer diagnosis, a crisis in a marriage or economic problems. This category will thus be treated very carefully here. Lazarus' categories of *loss*, *threat* and *challenge/gain* suggest that the seriousness of the situation and what must be done to rectify it are obvious to the subject. But this is not so. We cannot know the future, which often makes it difficult to decide what to do. This is true not only of the private problems of individuals, but also of the kinds of catastrophes modern societies are heir to, and people learn about through the media. The German sociologist Ulrich Beck (1986: 19-20) called this the 'Risk Society'. Through the media, new knowledge about all kinds of risks concerning health matters, crime, terror, accidents, climate change and so on is disseminated, showing everyone how dangerous life can be – though it is a historical truth that life in the Western world has never been safer, and people are living longer than they ever have before – sometimes even without diseases (Petersen et al., 2006). In spite of these facts insecurity and consciousness of risks are not being reduced – on the contrary. The modern human being does not believe in fate, but in individual acts as means to avoid accidents and early death, and this demands a high level of consciousness about all the risks we face (Hacking, 2010 [1990]). There is a whole industry of experts, consultants and self-help books about private economy, health, ecology and so on from which you can seek advice in your uncertainty. In some cases, we can act on statistical probabilities, building on historical figures (for instance, to calculate the risk of being in an aeroplane crash), and in other cases we must act on the advice of what we believe are reliable authorities.

Uncertainty in relation to private problems is also a typical type of burden and a condition that plays a role in the course of coping. When the objective situation is not clear, the perception of whether it can be changed will probably fluctuate throughout the coping course. This entails shifts in strategies and concrete problem-solving experiments, in a discursive process. A typical way of coping with uncertainty is to try several strategies in parallel in order to try to resolve as much as possible (problem-solving), and at the same time preparing oneself mentally for the worst (resignation; goal extinction) in parallel with palliative strategies that help one bear the uncertainty.

Such cases must be seen as especially burdensome because the unknowable future creates uncertainty about what to do – and by which means. These uncertain situations are typically seen in connection with illness: Am I going to live or die? Or will I become disabled? On the other hand, some people, especially those suffering from fatal diseases, are not interested in knowing more about their condition, but embrace uncertainty as a way of sustaining hope. Sometimes uncertainty is a hell, and sometimes it is a blessing.

Summary

It is necessary for the researcher to understand whether the subject believes it is possible to ameliorate their situation or not. Simply put: perceived reversibility will initiate problem-solving preventive and restorative processes in order to re-establish a status quo, while perceived irreversibility usually initiates mental changes such as active resignation or extinction of the value of the lost goal (see Chapter 1, and also Chapter 3). Very often the details are complicated by the fact that the subject is uncertain about what to do due to uncertainty about how things are. The consequence will typically be an attempt to save what can be saved and at the same time prepare oneself for the worst by using palliative strategies (see next section) in order to endure the uncertainty, which, conversely, may sometimes be embraced. This only shows the complexity of such cases.

4. EMOTIONAL REACTIONS

It is a psychological law that painful and conflicting so-called goal incongruent emotions arise in response to an experience of threatened or lost goals simply because their transactional meaning is changing. The character and intensity of an emotional reaction will depend on what precisely is at stake, and its position in the person's goal hierarchy. Here it is a good idea to repeat Nussbaum: an emotion always has an object.[40] For example, if the subject appraises a threat to their reputation, it will be the emotion of shame that is prominent in their reaction.

These emotional reactions will be a motive, alongside the burden itself, for coping – meaning they will be an object for palliative strategies, which do not target the burden, but aim to provide relief from the emotions caused by the burden. Palliative strategies aim to reduce emotions (anxiety, fear, grief, guilt, shame, jealousy, envy), provide an outlet for them (usually anger) or offer an escape from them (principally anxiety), and can take many forms. These strategies can in some cases comprise most of the coping course, for a matter of years if the problem is not solved. Palliative strategies can be observed, for example, among parents with disabled children, who experience the unpleasant emotion of guilt for having given birth to the child. Motives for coping are in such cases perhaps more about relieving a bad conscience than doing what is best for the development of the child, and may provoke protest and anger from the child. It is not difficult to imagine that it is easier to discipline a healthy child than a sick or disabled one, because there is already so much unhappiness in the relationship between the parents and the child. Palliative strategies can thus be rather short-sighted strategies, even whilst they allow everyday life to continue (see the case in Chapter 3).

It is surprising to see how much well-functioning people also use palliative strategies in parallel with strategies that aim to solve problems (Munk, 1999: 261–422). It is possible to imagine a dynamic coping course where palliative strategies play a bigger role at the beginning, eventually giving way to problem-solving and/or resignation strategies.

Summary

Aversive emotions seem in themselves to create a need for coping strategies – alongside the need to solve the problems, of course. Especially in long-term, painful coping courses it seems essential and even crucial to reduce emotional discomfort with palliative strategies. While such strategies do not solve the problem, whole patterns of them can grow throughout a coping course, establishing new life patterns for subjects.

5. RESOURCES OF PERSONALITY

The roles the different aspects of the coping course play naturally depend on what degree and in which form they are present. People with personal resources – including intelligence, a stable personality, no addiction and no disposition to becoming mentally ill – are better equipped to reach a certain level of control concerning their goals in life. This is not meant to be a normative point of view. But having a certain level of self-control and faculties for navigating life makes it more likely that one will experience a higher quality of life. On the other hand, robust and apparently privileged people can also experience problems and grief for which their resources are insufficient to allow them to cope.

Whether the situation is reversible or not – which is dependent on the objective character of the burden – many practical problems, and problems that the person has never encountered before, require some kind of solution. This demands cognitive resources such as:

- Reliable perception of the objective character of the burden;
- Ability to solve problems;
- A certain level of general knowledge;
- Insight into one's own abilities and limitations;
- A certain level of overview, initiative and ability to act; and
- Ability to find new ways of solving problems.

If the situation is absolutely irreversible, the ability to adapt to new conditions and see the potential for new goals in life to replace the lost ones is necessary for the person to regain their wellbeing.

The American cognitive psychologists Rybash, Hoyer and Roodin (1986) state that the ability to solve personal problems more or less depends on how one thinks about them. This is called *personal thinking style*. A comparison of two thinking styles and how these are expressed in relation to some dimensions of personal problems, can be seen in Table 3, which is reproduced from Rybash, Hoyer & Roodin (1986: 140). Rybash et al. differentiate between *formal* and *postformal* thinking styles, where the formal style is characterised by dogmatic and inflexible ways of thinking, which is considered to imply reduced ability to solve problems.[41] The informal thinking style, on the other hand, is open and more oriented towards finding innovative solutions. These categories should not be viewed as mutually exclusive, but more as opposites on a continuum along which personal thinking styles continually move.

Table 3. Solving personal problems: two different thinking styles

Relevant dimensions	Formal style	Postformal style
Perception of the character of personal problems	Problems are seen as entities which can be solved by logical analysis and in a formal way.	Problems are 'open' and can be solved by new informal solutions never seen before and through an understanding of the limitations of the logical analysis.
The relationship between thinking and emotion	Thinking is superior to emotions. Personal reasoning is looked upon as rational, but can be darkened and disturbed by emotions.	Personal reasoning represents recognition of thinking and feeling as integrated. Neither thinking nor feeling has precedence over one another.
Ways of coping	Distortion of reality, passive/defensive.	Acceptance of reality. Attempt to cope actively with the problems.

It is useful to remember that the narratives people produce in relation to their problems reveal the direction of their thinking, that is, whether they are formalists or non-formalists. You can thus achieve a sense of the person from the way they think about how difficult the coping process will be for them.

Other significant personal resources include maturity, self-confidence and a certain unconventional attitude to life, meaning that social norms do not dominate the way the person organises their life. The two thinking styles presented in Table 3 are related to the personality traits called 'rigidity' (formal style) and 'flexibility' (postformal style).[42]

The aspect of *emotional maturity* can very easily become normative and ethnocentric. Here it denotes the ability to endure pressure that causes unpleasant emotions and insecurity until better times come along, whether as a result of one's own strategies, an external intervention or a combination of the two.

Emotional insecurity, which is the opposite, leads to senseless attempts at problem-solving, which in unlucky cases can make the situation worse and begin a vicious circle. Emotional immaturity can also result in the overuse of palliative strategies that do not solve the fundamental problem. This can be destructive for mental health and quality of life. Finally, palliative strategies can sometimes ruin a person's health and undermine the possibilities for them to recover. The obvious example here is alcohol abuse.

Another example of emotional insecurity is running away from one's problems, without the dangerous implications of certain palliative strategies. More or less unconsciously it is possible to fail to confront one's problems; as a pattern of behaviour this is dysfunctional. Temporary ignorance or consciously 'parking' unpleasant thoughts outside one's attention can of course be a useful way of handling unpleasant emotions in situations where one does not know what the future will bring. As pointed out earlier, well-functioning people also use palliative strategies extensively in order to solve their problems better (Munk, 1999: 261–422).

Another relevant state is *emotional vulnerability*, understood here as a disposition to mental illness. Consequences include not only an unreliable perception of the objective character of the situation and of the self, and reduced ability to act, but also an aggravation of the whole situation. Expressed another way, the *absence* of disposition to mental illness (for example depression, psychoses, anxiety and personality disturbances) can in itself be a resource.

Competence at problem-solving and emotional (im-)maturity should be interpreted not only as innate faculties that are engaged, or not, at key points in a person's life. They are also resources that develop in transactions with a person's environment. Throughout life people learn about more or less constructive palliative strategies, such as physical exercise, music, alcohol and so on. Education, knowledge about the world and society in general and a certain level of belief in one's ability to cope are all the result of transactions with social environments in particular. This means that personal resources cannot be understood independent of a person's surroundings.

Summary

Personal faculties such as more or less advanced cognitive abilities, emotional maturity and hardiness are crucial for coping – whether the problems can be solved or not. Flexibility, knowledge, self-knowledge and ways of thinking about one's problems are a crucial dimension of cognitive ability, while the ability to endure emotional distress until things improve is critical to a person's capacity to act in relation to mental strain. Lack of emotional maturity and strength can very easily worsen the situation. Palliative strategies alone are not suitable because they do not solve problems; in combination with problem-solving strategies, however, they can help people to bear difficult situations.

6. ENVIRONMENTAL RESOURCES

From the perspective of coping, the question about environmental resources is not only about how the environment influences the development of a single person, making them more or less able to cope with adversity in life. The environment can also influence the problems of the person independent of their initiatives, in three different ways:

1. Positive intervention
2. Negative intervention
3. No intervention

The consequence of this fact is that – as very often repeated in this text – it is a mistake in analysing a coping course to focus only on the strategies of the person in question. Coping courses are influenced by social and material factors too – on a private level, such having good health,[43] and on a macrosocial level. The resources of the environment can intervene in a situation and/ or its consequences. Different interventions from public and private environments can in fact be a very dominant element in a coping course; outcomes are far from always a result of individual strategies (Pearlin, 1991; Munk, 1999). Practically and logically, these possible interventions should be affiliated to the concept of resources, and consequently also to the level of individual vulnerability. In other words: the kind of society you live in contributes to your level of individual resilience. These two aspects are very often completely separated in the research literature. It is sensible to claim that there is a significant relationship between access to resources and individual vulnerability. From an overall perspective of prevention, it can be said that human, micro-social and societal development all need to be considered as developing resources, because access to resources in a broad sense should increase the ability to control one's life.

> The basic assumption is that the richer the resources the richer the possibilities of managing the surrounding social and physical environment. This would lead to greater freedom of choice in manipulating the surrounding environment or in protecting oneself against unnecessarily being manipulated by the environment (Malmberg, 1991: 41).

The existence of resources is not only a help for persons in stressful situations but also preventative with respect to future such situations. Today it is a well-documented fact that illness in general, including illnesses due to lifestyle that cause early death, is statistically connected with low socioeconomic status, low level of education and poor health.[44]

Not only does a rich diversity of resources prevent diverse types of problems even occurring, but it also contributes to recovery following losses. The meaning of a distressing situation is a question not only of having personal goals at stake, but also of access to help. The Israeli sociologist A. Antonovsky (1985) discusses the importance of resources in relation to problems of distress. He talks about *generalised resources of resistance*, which can be transformed into specific resources or aids in order to resolve or ameliorate a situation of mental strain. These generalized resources include – according to Antonovsky – all kinds of characteristics of a person, a group or an environment that can contribute to the effective reduction of mental strain. He considers the differences between persons and groups as primarily differences in distribution of these general resources of resistance.

Resources of resistance include a plurality of qualitatively different types of resources from different sources: the body, the psyche, the culture and macro-, meso- or micro-social circumstances. Antonovsky defines distress as a state characterised by an absence of resources or a breakdown in the buffers of the general resources of resistance that protect the subject. On the other hand, he considers life benign when those general resources of resistance are present. This should, according to Antonovsky, create a sense of coherence in the subject, as well as positive expectations about life, a belief in stability and a certain predictability. General resources of resistance make a positive difference to a person's quality of life, as well as fighting, in their more specific forms, a plurality of sources of distress. Antonovsky defines the characteristics of these forms on different levels of the world of the subject, which is the source of specific resources.

In terms of the body, this is about susceptibility and resistance to nefarious aspects of the physical environment, including biochemical immunity, on the physiological and anatomical level.

According to Antonovsky, a similar type of flexibility is seen in a person's mind; a certain measure of intelligence, emotional maturity,[45] and independence from prevailing norms increases the likelihood a person will be able to cope – and perhaps even generally to do well in life. Antonovsky is here in line with Rybash, Hoyer and Roodin's characteristics of the 'good coper' (1986) or the postformal coper (see Table 3).

On the interpersonal level, close relations – created by mutual engagements – are important social resources. Another potent resource is wrapped up in culture, which provides rules and frameworks for how to cope with an array of demands in life, for example death. Culture gives us resources such as language, norms and a place in the world, supplementing innate mental plasticity with structure or direction. Finally, material wealth is also a resource which – apart from catering to immediate physical and mental needs – can open doors to solutions of all kinds of problems.[46]

Summary

Access to external help in a situation of mental strain can be crucial in solving problems – whether economic, health or emotional issues. Resources help people keep and restore control over their lives. Resources can be collectively or politically organised, for example free medical care or economic help; they can also be private, such as personal savings, or a social network that can be mobilised if needed. The outcomes of most coping courses cannot be explained only by individual strategies. As a researcher, you must also look out for the help and support offered to a person by their environment. Antonovsky, who is particularly interested in the prevention of illness, emphasises that all kinds of resources in the external environment as well as in the mind of the person also contribute to the prevention of illnesses.

Coping courses are dependent on many things. This chapter provides the user of the manual with a wider perspective on current forms of coping analysis, encouraging reflection on the resources informants have access to when they are in trouble.

CHAPTER 3

GUIDANCE ON THE ANALYSIS OF COPING COURSES

In the following section the concepts and the process template (Table 4) for analysing the coping interview will be explained. It may seem strange to do things in this order, since the interview is the origin of the material for the analysis mentioned in earlier sections. One should be quite clear, however, about the focus of the coping interview. The deeper your understanding of the concepts and terminology, the more reliable you become as an interviewer.

As part of the explanation of the method I will demonstrate the meaning and use of the concepts in each of the six columns in table 4 with a constructed but realistic case about a man who experiences a social redirection as a consequence of unemployment. In this way it is possible to see how categorisation by numbers and letters is done in the analysis. Furthermore, I will demonstrate the method with an example from my own research: a woman with a husband suffering from dementia, whom she does not love. Here the objective problems are completely different from those of the constructed case: the woman's coping course is about her battle with herself and with her feelings of guilt and shame.

Before explaining how the scheme should be filled in, it is worth stating that the interview must be recorded and transcribed in full in order to complete the analysis. A reliable coping analysis cannot be conducted on the basis of listening to a recording or reading notes made during the interview. As mentioned in the next chapter's section about memory and personal recollections, the researcher should not assume that the relevant information will emerge nicely, in chronological order. Usually, on the surface an interview appears messy, and jumps in and out of the informant's memories. In the analysis, it is important to restore the chronology of causes or important events. You may begin by describing a chronological course in the column to the left and afterwards filling out the columns one at a time (Table 4). This demands that you read back and forth in the transcription – often many times – in order to identify the information meant for every column in the scheme.[47] After that, mark the categories that go together throughout the scheme to produce an organised and coherent narrative of the difficult period in the life of the informant. In the detailed guidance about how to fill out the scheme, the marks are mentioned together with the relevant columns. Do this at the same time as you input the categories and control to match the different parts throughout the scheme, so that it is possible for you to detect a coherent process or coping course. This should not be understood, however, as a picture of real life being orderly unchaotic. The order in the scheme should mirror the interface between the event and what happens over time in and for the person who is coping with something.

The structure of the scheme is separated into columns (Table 4), each of which are meant to cover an analytical category that will help the researcher achieve an overview of the coping process. As mentioned above, this can seem quite rigid but should not be understood as a direct picture of the process and its mutual and usually very complex interplay between the appraisals, emotions and acts of the coping person. This interplay is instead pictured by the letters and numbers marked on the information in the scheme.

But the structure of the scheme and its concepts is one thing; drawing out the relevant information from the interviews and translating this into the analytic language of the scheme is something else entirely. This latter task is only learnt with patience, and I recommend that at first you do the analysis in a group, allowing for discussions about doubts and generally making the

work more interesting. Regarding finding and extracting information, you should follow this process:

- PREPARATION: Read the transcription
  - Read the whole interview very thoroughly.
  - Reread it – perhaps several times – in order to localise the
    information relevant to the six columns of the scheme.

- STEP ONE: Identify the distressing event(s) (column 1)
  - Find the distressing events pointed out by the
    informant and mark them with a sequence number
    in the transcription.
  - Write the events into the first column in chronological
    order, with their sequence numbers (see Tables 4 and 5).
    The events retain their numbers across the scheme so
    that you can follow interpretations, emotional reactions
    and so on as they occur in connection with the event.
    This also allows you to sort out the succession and
    perhaps messy integration of events, appraisals,
    reactions, acts and perhaps interventions.

- STEP TWO: Find the personal meanings (column 2)
  - Find the personal meaning connected to each burden,
    and decide whether it is interpreted as a *threat*, *loss*
    or *challenge* (or, indeed, a gain in some way)
    (see Tables 4 and 6).
  - Give each meaning the number of the distressing event
    to which it belongs to, and add lower-case letters so
    that you can see how meanings are connected with each
    event. The order of these letters does not matter, but
    only that all of them are registered. Follow the same
    procedure for each distressing event pointed out by
    the informant (see Table 6).

- STEP THREE: Estimate the emotional implications (column 3)
  - Estimate the emotional implications related to the different personal meanings: *threat, loss, challenge* or *gain* and write them into column three.
  - Label the emotional reactions with the same numbers and letters as the personal meanings to which they are attached (see Tables 4 and 7).

It may be that you cannot detect what the informant is feeling from what they say. Instead you must interpret or 'translate' from what is actually said. You must always, however, have good arguments when you interpret in this way.

- STEP FOUR: Map the coping strategies used by the informant (column 4)
  - Map the coping strategies and estimate which are used in relation to each personal meaning and/or emotion, then write them into the scheme (see Tables 4, 8, 25 and 26).
  - Give to each strategy the same number and letter as the personal meaning and/or emotion to which it corresponds. If you find more than one strategy corresponding to the same personal meaning and/or emotion, the sequence will be, for example, 2.a.1, 2.a.2, 2.a.3 and so on. This makes it clear that they apply to the same emotion (a) and/or meaning (the first number 2), but are different coping strategies. This also means that you will be able to see the sequence in which they were used in the case (see Table 25).
  - Make sure you also note in column four which *concrete* acts the strategies encompass. This is partly a control for the interpretations of the researcher, and partly an indication of the concrete situation of the informant. If you do not do this, the danger is that the analysis becomes too vague, abstract and short of information for understanding what is really happening to the person.

- STEP 5: Identify interventions (column 5)
  - If any interventions (positive and/or negative) occurred in the case, they should be written into column five.
  - If the intervention is a help in the situation, give it the same number and letter of the distressing event and personal meaning it influences, as shown in the constructed case, where relatives intervene to help the person experiencing mental strain (see Table 27).
  - Record the exact nature of the intervention in the same column.
  - Negative interventions should be given a new initial number in the chronological sequence of distressing events and recorded in both column one (as a new burden) and column five (as an intervention), where they should also be numbered according to the initial distressing event and personal meaning they influence (see Table 27). In this way, you can see from the scheme that we are dealing with both a new burden and a negative intervention into an old one (or multiple old ones).

You can always ask the informant – of course – whether something is actually a new burden, or only a negative influence on the old one. In the constructed but very realistic case below, you will find examples of both: new direct changes in the situation, as for example the subject's house being ordered to be sold by the court, are new distressing events, while a high level of unemployment in society in connection with the subject's redundancy is a negative intervention.

- STEP 6: record the outcomes of each sub-process (column 6)
  - Note down: What *changes* have occurred? Has the burden *disappeared*? Have *new* burdens appeared? What is the subject's *quality of life* in relation to their *moods* and *mental ability to function*? Has the person *changed their self-perception* and/or *perception of their environment*? Have there been any *changes of roles*? Or any changes at the *physical, social, material and economic levels*? Or changes in the person's *daily life*? (See Table 28.)
  - Again, describe the changes concretely too.

- STEP 7: Detect patterns across cases
  - After the analysis of each interview in the project is done, attempt to detect patterns within each case, and also across cases. What similarities are there between the personal meanings, emotional reactions and so on among the individuals in the group? Where are the differences, and what might be their causes?

This categorisation of the informants' description of their experiences is a work of patience – but it is also exciting, because it is here that you will obtain a deeper insight into their motives, and what is at stake in their situations of distress: the very focus of your research project. It is likely you will detect new perspectives that you had not seen during the interviews. Both the interview and the coping analysis are processes of detection.

It is recommended that you use an A3 copy of the scheme shown in Table 4 on which to record your analysis. Each interview should be analysed on a separate scheme.

Table 4. Scheme for the analysis of the coping course

Record the informant's gender, age, education, profession and marital status

Time	**Column 1** The distressing event(s)	**Column 2** Personal meaning	**Column 3** Emotional implications
Units of analysis	*Event*	*Threat* *Loss* *Challenge* *Gain*	*Grief* *Anger* *Envy* *Jealousy* *Contempt* *Anxiety* *Fear* *Shame* *Guilt* *Relief* *Hope* *Gratitude* *Compassion* *Happiness/joy* *Pride* *Love*

Column 4 Coping strategies	Column 5 Interventions	Column 6 Outcomes
Status quo *Restoration* *Prevention*	*Positive or* *Negative* *intervention*	Is the mental strain gone? Changed roles? Have new burdens appeared?
Change *Active resignation* *Extinction of goal*		Changes in health, social relations (apart from roles), material and economic status?
Palliation		Quality of life: mood and mental functioning
-------- *(Passive resignation)*		Changed perception of self and environment Changes in everyday life?

Constructed case to demonstrate the analysis

The person is a 40-year-old man, married with children. He is sacked from his work. He enjoyed his work life and liked his colleagues, but had a negative relationship with his manager. He was dependent on his income from his job, but has not succeeded in finding a new job, and the new family house was ordered to be sold by the court because he could longer pay for it. These circumstances created tensions in his marriage, which led to divorce.

The analysis of this constructed case will be short, because it does not build on the categorisation of an interview with a real person.

STEP ONE: Identify the distressing event(s)

Table 5. Column 1: Distressing events

Distressing event(s) (constructed case)
1. Sacked from job
2. House forced on sale
3. Divorce

Explanation of column 1: distressing event(s)

The events pointed out by the subject for the period investigated by the researcher are listed here in chronological order. The short descriptions of the events should be as neutral and objective as possible – that is, not coloured by the subject's appraisal of them. Neutrally-described events allow for comparisons of informants who have experienced the same type of event. They can also contribute to an understanding of the coping course, including any limitations on the ability of the subject to act to solve their problems. In this constructed case, the subject needs more money, but he has no way of earning any.

The distressing events should be numbered chronologically, so that you can follow the subject's interpretations of and reactions to each event, as well as trace the progress of the coping course from the initial event. This is necessary for systematic analysis (see Table 5).

STEP TWO: Find the personal meanings

Table 6. Column 2: Personal meanings

Distressing event(s)	Personal meanings
1. Sacked from job	1.a Loss of relationships with good colleagues
	1.b Loss of daily occupation
	1.c Loss of social recognition
	1.d Loss of authority as the breadwinner of the family
	1.e Threat to family's finances
	1.f Threat to marital harmony
	1.g Profit: freedom from an unpleasant relationship with manager
2. House forced on sale	2.a Loss of home
	2.b Loss of social recognition
	2.c Loss of harmonious family life
3. Divorce	3.a Loss of spouse
	3.b Profit: freedom from difficult relationship with spouse
	3.c Loss of daily contact with children
	3.d Loss of daily life with family
	3.e Loss of satisfaction with life

Explanation of column 2: personal meanings

The subject's personal interpretation of what happened is the focus of the analysis because it expresses the harm or threat of harm that is the ultimate goal of the restorative process. The core analytical concepts here are *threat*, *loss* (which may be temporary), *challenge* and *profit*. The subject's emotions and actions are subsequently directed by this interpretation, which expresses what exactly is at stake for the person in relation to their goal hierarchy. Analysing personal meanings thus also helps the researcher to identify all the goals towards which the coping process is directed. Which goals are under threat, vulnerable to loss or temporary loss or in conflict with each other? Are there any gains to be had in connection with the losses, as seen in the constructed case (where losing a job means freedom from an unpleasant relationship with a manager)?

These personal meanings are given letters after the number of the distressing event with which they are associated (see Table 6). This helps distinguish the meanings of different events, which obviously constitute different coping motives.

STEP THREE: Estimate the emotional implications

Table 7. Column 3: Emotional implications

Distressing event(s)	Personal meanings	Emotional implications
1. Sacked from job	1.a Loss of relationships with good colleagues	1.a Grief, low spirits, anger
	1.b Loss of daily occupation	1.b Grief, sadness
	1.c Loss of social recognition	1.c Shame
	1.d Loss of authority as the breadwinner of the family	1.d Shame, guilt
	1.e Threat to family's finances	1.e Fear, anxiety
	1.f Threat to marital harmony	1.f Anger, anxiety, hope
	1.g Profit: freedom from an unpleasant relationship with manager	1.g Relief
2. House forced on sale	2.a Loss of home	2.a Grief, low spirits, guilt
	2.b Loss of social recognition	2.b Shame
	2.c Loss of harmonious family life	2.c Grief, guilt, anger

Distressing event(s)	Personal meanings	Emotional implications
3. Divorce	3.a Loss of spouse	3.a Grief
	3.b Profit: freedom from difficult relationship with spouse	3.b Relief
	3.c Loss of daily contact with children	3.c Grief, sadness, guilt
	3.d Loss of daily life with family	3.d Grief, sadness
	3.e Loss of satisfaction with life	3.e Depression (this is not a solitary emotion, but a complex clinical state)

Explanation of column 3: emotional implications

Filling out column three demands a lot of preparation in order to become confident with the 16 different emotions of the coping analysis. These will be explained in the following, but first let us take a look at the concept of 'emotions' more generally.

The emotional implications of personally relevant events are an instrument of understanding for the researcher and also, of course, for the subject. Quite often it is not at all obvious to us why we react emotionally as we do; emotional reactions come before conscious cognitive insight into our mental states, and therefore tell us something different about ourselves. This also means that we can be surprised by our own emotional reactions, as we do not always consciously know every aspect of our goal hierarchies. Returning to Nussbaum's dictum (2004) that emotions always have an object: emotional reactions reveal something important about a relationship between a subject and some object in their world – a relationship that is not always clear to the subject.

It can be difficult for the subject to identify exactly why they find an event distressing, and in many cases, it is easier to 'read' their emotions directly. Emotions disclose the relational meaning of a transaction and thus can be considered to be 'rational', though not in the way this word is usually understood.[48] Emotional rationality refers not to traditional logics, but to the *character of our relationships*, and as such it is an important means to self-understanding. Emotions have an internal logic, even if we normally call them 'irrational'. Speaking about an individual's values and existential problems presupposes the existence of emotions and the ability to feel comfort and discomfort. Each emotion includes a narrative about what is specifically at stake for the person: Lazarus calles this a *core relational* theme.

Emotions are not a complex of diverse states: a single emotion cannot be divided into simpler units. It is not a simple task, however, to decide whether something we think belongs to a category is in fact indivisible. This demands well-argued criteria for such a categorisation.[49] Lazarus resolved this with a category he called 'unsecure' emotions – for those instances where the researcher cannot be sure they are dealing with a clearly delimited and indivisible emotion. One example is 'hope'. Hope is included in this manual's categorisation; it is defined as a future-oriented emotion associated with desperate circumstances and consequently also with coping. Furthermore, our language for emotional states is rich and varied, which further complicates the problems of working in this difficult field. The researcher's criteria must stand up to analysis. To further complicate things, Lazarus also discusses 'variations' of the emotions (Lazarus, 1991; 215–296), which include levels of intensity: I may be a bit annoyed, or I may be so absorbed with furiousness that I cannot control myself.

In spite of the difficulties of analysing emotions, this author finds that the 16 emotions Lazarus demarcates are useful tools in understanding the reactions of a person experiencing stress.[50]

Lazarus states that an emotion may be defined by the following criteria (Lazarus, 1991: 215–296):

1. *A core relational theme* which is specific to each emotion.
2. *A pattern of appraisal* ('if-then') which follows the scheme in Table 1. If there is *goal incongruence* then any *unpleasant* emotion is possible; if there is *goal congruence*, any *pleasant* emotion is possible; the same applies if the coping potential and expectations of the future are favourable or unfavourable.
3. *An – unspecific – physiological reaction* which can be everything from a high level of tension in the body with blushing and a pounding heart or to the contrary, for example the paralysis often seen in people mourning.
4. *A tendency to act*, for example an incentive for revenge due to an anger which cannot be expressed for reasons of propriety. To mention an obvious example: you may feel an incentive to kill someone, but do not do it because the cost to yourself would be too high.

As shown in the example about anger, human beings have the ability to repress emotional impulses for reasons of social propriety.[51] Lazarus' concept of emotions includes the whole narrative of the body and mind regarding a person's trajectory through the turbulence of life. He also adds that each emotion can in theory develop into a pathological state, becoming part of a permanent mental state so that it can be considered as a personality trait. This is important to remember when evaluating the outcome of a coping process. Has anger developed into 'bitterness'? Has anxiety developed into a constant nervousness, or a manifest disturbance of personality? Usually you will see many different kinds of emotional reactions in a transaction, which shows that many kinds of relational meanings are at work. The researcher must identify and differentiate them, using every-

thing they know about the criteria for each emotion. Lazarus'
16 emotions are grouped thus (Lazarus, 1999: 210–255):[52]

A. Socially 'unpleasant' emotions: *anger* and its variants,
   such as *envy, jealousy* and *contempt*
B. Existential emotions: *anxiety, fear, guilt* and *shame*
C. Emotions provoked by unpleasant life experiences:
   relief, hope and *grief*
D. Empathetic emotions: *gratitude* and *sympathy*
C. Emotions provoked by pleasant life experiences:
   joy, pride and *love*

Analysing emotions is important not only because it helps the
researcher to understand the personal meanings that are the
foundation of a coping process; unpleasant emotions such as
anxiety or guilt can also constitute separate motives for coping.
This is especially the case when the fundamental problem does
not have an immediate solution. The phenomenon can be seen
in the case of the wife caring for a demented spouse, and this
can grow into a total life pattern.[53]

   The 16 emotions isolated by Lazarus will be explained in the
following in terms of their core relational themes, tendency to
motivate action, linguistic expression and pathological types.
Unpleasant or negative emotions will always be dominant in a
coping analysis. However, since turbulent life events can in principle also entail unforeseen, positive outcomes, the ensuing
emotional reactions are also included in the analysis. Apart from
a few additions made by me (mentioned in the text), the following overview of emotions is built on Lazarus' categorisations
(Lazarus, 1991: part 3; 1999).

A: Socially unpleasant emotions

Table 8. Anger

Core relational theme	Degrading treatment/ offence that threatens one's ego identity[54]
Action tendency	Incentive for revenge
Other expressions for anger	Rage, violence, indignation, irritation, hatred, sarcasm, bad temper, hostility, desperation, bitterness, indignation, obstinacy, resentment, sourness, malice, revenge, irritability, contempt (notice the differences in intensity)
Pathology	Physical and mental violence against others; domestic abuse patterns; permanent bitterness and disillusion; inclination to perceive insults everywhere; lack of ability to control anger

Table 9. Envy

Core relational theme	Desire for something that others have
Action tendency	Impulse to obtain the wished-for thing
Other expressions for envy	Desire, greed
Pathology	Perception of self as unlucky and/or victimised

Table 10. Jealousy

Core relational theme	Anger directed at a third party because of a threat to or loss of another person's affection
Action tendency	Attempt to make oneself more 'loveable' to the other and/or take revenge against the third party (the competitor), literally and/or symbolically
Other expressions for jealousy	Envy, suspiciousness, 'the green-eyed monster'
Pathology	Jealousy can objectively be well founded, but when it is pathological the person constantly demands assurances of fidelity

Table 11. Disgust

Core relational theme	Distaste. Not a biological impulse but a learned and ideologically conditioned reaction
Action tendency	A strong impulse to avoid contact with the disapproved object or the unpalatable idea (in some respects this looks like nausea)
Other expressions for disgust	Contempt, aversion, antipathy
Pathology	Lazarus' psychoanalytical interpreetation: 'Here contempt is closely related to anxiety of sexuality, aggression and death and is connected to ideas about damaging, evil and "unclean" parts of oneself (concretely and symbolically) and of the horror of helplessness, castration, death and decay' (Lazarus, 1991: 262).

B: Existential emotions

Table 12. Anxiety

Core relational theme	An unspecified existential threat from an unknown source
Action tendency	Since the cause is unspecified, it is not possible to remove it or escape from it; palliative strategies are the only option,ranging from distraction techniques to drugs.
Other expressions for anxiety	Worry, nervousness, panic, fright, unease, concern, apprehension, worry, horror
Pathology	Panic and generalized anxiety[55]

Table 13. Fear

Core relational theme	A concrete and sudden, but recognisable, threat
Action tendency	Escape or fight the immediate danger
Other expressions for fear	Horror, fright, uneasiness, 'anxiety',[56] consternation, dismay
Pathology	Phobic and obsessive-compulsive states (OCD)[57]

Table 14. Shame

Core relational theme	Failure to live up to an ego-ideal of recognition from valued others; a thought or real witness is required to release the emotion
Action tendency	Incentive to hide one's failure, particularly from people who are important to the subject
Other expressions for shame	Humiliation, shyness, feeling, stupid, 'losing face', remorse, regret, embarrassment
Pathology	Over-sensitivity; defensive actions to reduce exposure to situations that might end in humiliation; exaggerated perfectionism, permanent anxiety, self-remorse and negative self-perception; lack of judgement in social situations; lack of self-esteem; suicidal feelings[58]

Table 15. Guilt

Core relational theme	A feeling of having violated one's own moral imperative; the thought alone is enough to provoke the reaction – no witness is needed
Action tendency	Penance towards the person one feels one has wronged, who may not even know they are affected and may be pleased by the attention[59]
Other expressions for guilt	Bad conscience, responsibility, accountability, remorse
Pathology	Depression; suicidal thoughts;[60] perfectionism, permanent anxiety, self-remorse and a negative self-image; reduced judgement in social situations

C: Emotions provoked by life circumstances appraised as unfavourable[61]

Table 16. Relief

Core relational theme	Presupposes a goal-incongruent – threatening – event that has reduced or disappeared, e.g. a message from a doctor that one's test results show nothing is wrong
Action tendency	Tension disappears from the body along with readiness to act (grief and relief are the only emotions where the tendency to act is connected with a fall in the curve of tension)
Other expressions for relief	Encouragement, reassurance, consolation, comfort, solace, calmness, relaxation, repose, ease
Pathology	None

Table 17. Hope[62]

Core relational theme	Longing (sometimes desperate) after improvement of a threatening, awful outcome of a situation ('Fear the worst and hope for the best')
Action tendency	Permanently alert and engaged in a heavily wished-for outcome, even if the prospects look very bad[63]
Other expressions for hope	Aspiration, desire, wish, expectation, ambition, aim, plan, dream, daydream, pipe dream, longing, yearning, craving, hankering
Pathology	Suppression of obvious but unpleasant realities

Table 18. Grief

Core relational theme	An irreversible loss
Action tendency	Withdrawal from 'the world'/ inactivity in relation to the loss
Other expressions for grief	Unhappiness, misery, melancholy, sadness
Pathology	Depression and risk of suicide; inclination to be nostalgic, a bittersweet condition

D: Empathetic emotions

Table 19. Gratitude

Core relational theme	Appreciation of an (unexpected?) altruistic gift
Action tendency	Incentive to show kindness to the donor; perhaps a wish to pay them back in some way
Other expressions for gratitude	Obligation, debt, appreciation
Pathology	An exaggerated feeling of debt – to the limits of dependency

Table 20. Compassion

Core relational theme	To be moved by the sufferings of another person, with a wish to help
Action tendency	Impulse to relieve another's condition, to help, to express sympathy
Other expressions for compassion	Empathy, sympathy, kindness, concern, consideration, condolence
Pathology	1. Lack of ability to express balanced compassion because the person is so overwhelmed by the situation (mostly seen among close relatives of the person suffering) 2. Lack of ability to feel compassion due to burnout or dehumanised narratives about the suffering person 3. Purely 'cognitive' compassion, without any emotional participation at all, as seen in psychopathy 4. Compassion that 'mirrors' another's suffering, with no ability to step back from the situation, as seen in some cases of autism[64]

E: Emotions provoked by life circumstances appraised as favourable

Table 21. Happiness/Joy

Core relational theme	Obvious progress in the realisation of goals in a generally positive life situation
Action tendency	Incentive to share one's good fortune with others; when the cause is the efforts of the subject or people close to them, a tendency to brag or boast may be seen
Other expressions for happiness/joy	Wellbeing, satisfaction, pleasure, fun, enjoyment, delight, amusement
Pathology	Bragging can be used to support a weak ego identity, that is, personal insecurity; it may also manifest in self-importance and pomposity; permanent and compulsive happiness, as seen in states of hypomania and 'smiling' depressions (where the person does not immediately seem depressed)

Table 22. Pride

Core relational theme	Achieving a highly-valued goal, either for the subject themselves or for a person or group with which they identify
Action tendency	An incentive to share the news with everyone (the opposite of shame)
Other expressions for pride	Triumph, satisfaction, arrogance
Pathology	Bragging can be used to support a weak ego identity, that is, personal insecurity; it may also manifest in self-importance and pomposity

Table 23. Romantic love

Core relational theme	Affection for another person (not necessarily reciprocal)
Tendency of action	Incentive to experience mental and physical, including sexual, intimacy with the loved one, and to show tenderness, interest and care
Other expressions for romantic love	Admiration, attraction, passion, fire, desire, affection, tenderness
Pathology	Reduced ability to give up a non-reciprocal relationship. Obsession with the loved one, perhaps resulting in a stalking process; another possibility is an unconscious attempt to reconstruct a parent–child relationship in a romantic relationship (dominance, distance, dependence or ambivalence)

Table 24. Parental and platonic love

Core relational theme	Affection for another person, not necessarily reciprocal
Tendency of action	Incentive to experience mental and physical intimacy with the loved one, and to show tenderness, interest and care
Other expressions for parental and platonic love	Affection, care, tenderness, concern
Pathology	Failure to adapt one's affection to changes in the loved one's life, e.g. a child becoming more independent and autonomous

Table 25. Column 4: coping strategies

Distressing event(s)	Personal meanings	Emotional implications	Coping strategies
1. **Sacked** **from job**	1.a Loss of relationship with good colleagues	1.a Grief, low spirits, anger	1.a Passive resignation
	1.b Loss of daily occupation	1.b Grief, sadness	1.b Passive resignation
	1.c Loss of social recognition	1.c Shame	1.c Palliative strategy: concealment; does not tell anyone outside the family
	1.d Loss of authority as the breadwinner of the family	1.d Shame, guilt	1.d Palliative strategy: hiding behind the TV (shame); shows penance (guilt): doing more practical work in the home (this is also a restorative strategy in relation to 1.b Loss of daily occupation)
	1.e Threat to family's finances	1.e Fear, anxiety	1.e Attempt to restore the situation: seeking work, reducing costs in the household
	1.f Threat to marital harmony	1.f Anger, anxiety, hope	1.f Palliative strategy (anger) and attempt to restore the situation: expressing anger at his wife in hope of making her reduce her spending
	1.g Profit: freedom from an unpleasant relationship with manager	1.g Relief	

Distressing event(s)	Personal meanings	Emotional implications	Coping strategies
2. **House forced on sale**	2.a Loss of home	2.a Grief, low spirits, guilt	2.a.1 Passive resignation
			2 a.2 Attempt at restoration: looking for a new home for the family
	2.b Loss of social recognition	2.b Shame	2.b Palliative strategy: does not talk about the situation
	2.c Loss of harmonious family life	2.c Grief, guilt, anger	2.c.1 Palliative (anger) and restorative strategy: reproach wife for lack of solidarity 2.c.2 Palliative strategy (guilt), shows penance: pays more attention to the children, even spoiling them
3. **Divorce**	3.a Loss of spouse	3.a Grief	3.a Passive resignation
	3.b Profit: freedom from difficult relationship with spouse	3.b Relief	
	3.c Loss of daily contact with children	3.c Grief, sadness, guilt	3.c.1 Passive resignation 3.c.2 Palliative strategy, penance (guilt): spoiling children with sweets and films
	3.d Loss of daily life with family	3.d Grief, sadness	3.d Passive resignation
	3.e Loss of satisfaction with life	3.e Depression (This is not a solitary emotion, but a complex clinical state)	3.e Passive resignation: Attempts suicide

Explanation of column 4: Coping strategies

In Table 25 an overview is given of possible strategies and their respective functions. It should be repeated here that the strategies:

- are defined by their *function* in relation to the threatened or damaged relationship and *not* by the act in itself;
- are mutually exclusive; and
- cover all kinds of concrete coping acts in relation to threat, loss and challenges (see also Table 2).

When analysing these strategies, it is important to maintain one's focus on the perspective of the informant, due to the close relationship between personal meanings and coping.

Table 26. Types of coping strategy and their function

Type of strategy (Column 4 in Table 4)	Function
Prevention and restoration	Prevention of permanent changes of the relationship and restoration to status quo (only in cases where a loss appears to be temporary). No change of the goal hierachy.
Active resignation (nobody is responsible for the loss)	Reduction of expectations about the transaction, and thus no change of the goal hierarchy, but there is no longer any possibility of realising the lost goal.
Extinction of value/goal: removal of a goal from the goal hierarchy (usually somebody is responsible)	Change in emotional engagement with the goal leading to its removal from the goal hierarchy.
Palliation	Relief from unpleasant emotions (though nothing is done to remove the fundamental problem).
Passive resignation	Nothing is done at all.

NARRATIVITY AND COPING STRATEGIES

As mentioned earlier, each type of coping strategy is followed by specific narratives. According to the American sociologist L. Richardson (1990), a narrative is a way in which a person organises their experiences, and is associated with local contexts where specific connections between episodes in the person's life can be pointed out and explained. Narrativity can be used to establish meaningful explanations of experiences, and they are integrated into the discourses of daily life. This creates connections and meaning in life – even when we find ourselves powerless to affect the narrative. Knowledge of characteristic narratives is also useful in interpreting figures of speech that are affiliated with the problems you detect in your research. Research findings can thus be 'translated' into common turns of phrase, reducing the distance between the abstract universe of research terminology and common knowledge.

In the following sections, more explanations of the strategy types and the specific narratives that follow them are given.

THE COPING STRATEGIES 'PREVENTION' AND 'RESTORATION'

Prevention and restoration strategies are both efforts to avoid the fact that essential conditions are changing. They both also operate with the same logic as classic problem-solving. Prevention strategies are built on the premise that something bad will happen unless something is done about it, which is possible. This is only a threat. However, a temporary loss is also a possibility, in which case restoration to the status quo is possible, avoiding any permanent change.

Sometimes a perceived threat cannot be avoided. Aside from removing the threat, prevention and restoration strategies also have an indirectly palliative effect, as emotional troubles are removed along with the problems. It is not difficult to isolate problem-solving activities in the coping interview; if the problem is illness, the informant seeks medical help, and if the problem is lack of money, the solution is to try to earn more or save money if possible. However, prevention and restoration can also imply complicated coping courses demanding vast effort from the person. In other cases, the subject may experience a stroke of luck, understood as a kind of intervention on the part of fate. The researcher will usually identify a narrative about a heroic effort or a 'lucky strike', which averted catastrophe.

THE COPING STRATEGY 'ACTIVE RESIGNATION'

While the problem-solving strategies treated in the former section aim to change external conditions, active resignation strategies are focused on changing the attitude of the person with the problem. An irreversible loss cannot be an object for restoration; if the person is going to 'survive' the loss and regain their quality of life, they need to recognise the loss as a reality and slowly get accustomed to it. These processes are always followed in the interview by narratives with a specific structure. In cases of active resignation, there is what I call a 'resigned' or 'comforting' narrative. One decisive precondition for this strategy is that the informant is not able to blame anyone for the loss. This would create anger and guilt, making it more difficult to get through the experience.

The elements of the narrative all have an obvious self-comforting function. In this process of change the love for the lost object does not disappear; instead, there is a reduction of expectations in order to realise a concrete life under the new conditions. In other words, no reprioritising of the goal hierarchy takes place. The narrative of resignation explains why and how the person has to change tracks in relation to the loss. It is typically divided into three parts, all of which are usually easy to find in the interview:

1. Acquittal: explaining why the loss happened and that the attached person is not to blame – in fact nobody is to be blamed (for example: 'This is natural; my husband has passed away because he was old').
2. Paradox: understanding that the alternative would have been worse; so the loss was actually a blessing ('It was a happy thing that he passed away, because his life would have become terrible if he had gone on living').
3. After all: looking forward to the future by recognising that life is still worth living ('Luckily I have my health, lovely children, money in the bank, etc.').

The narrative of resignation is primarily seen in connection with loss when someone dies. There is no assault of the ego-identity. The most important element in being able to continue one's life without being tormented by guilt is relief due to nobody can be blamed – point one above. In this narrative anger and guilt are excluded. The subject does not perceive themselves to have damaged their own moral imperatives in thought or action in connection with the loss; neither do they blame anyone else. An active resignation process is difficult to accomplish if guilt, anger or bitterness are associated with the loss. However, the two other elements of the active process of resignation are just as significant: positive reformulation of the loss and an ability to think positively about the future, too. In your research you will hear narratives that only show one of these elements or perhaps only two of the three, and here the mourning process is more difficult. At the same time, it is important to recognise that a full narrative of resignation does not prevent grief, but only helps ensure that the subject will live through the crisis without pathological reactions. A full narrative will sometimes be formulated very soon after the loss – even when the person is very unhappy – which should be seen as a predictor that the process of grief will not become pathological.

THE COPING STRATEGY 'EXTINCTION OF GOAL'

An alternative process of change may take place in connection with a loss, one that can be difficult to differentiate from *personal meaning*. The lost object or goal loses its value to the subject, and is thus removed as a goal from the goal hierarchy. In the scheme this is called *extinction of value/goal*. This phenomenon is primarily seen in connection with mental strain that is powerfully attacking the ego-identity, for example in cases of deceit. The difference between this and active resignation is that here the goal hierarchy is changed, and that someone is to blame. The process is followed by what could be called a *narrative of extinction*, which deconstructs the goal. Some reconstruction of the past will be integrated into the narrative, since the events of the present will have changed the subject's perspective of what happened before. This process is primarily about the subject's perceptions of the blameworthy person (which may be themselves) and is marked by grief, anger and bitterness. During the interview the researcher will be able to identify an often violently changed opinion of the relationship.

THE COPING STRATEGY 'PALLIATION'

Aversive emotions, primarily anxiety, can be a motive in themselves. The characteristic of anxiety is that the cause of the threat is not known; since it is thus difficult to know what to do to counteract the threat, the only option is to target the anxiety. Guilt can also be a frequent provocation for palliative strategies, for example penance (see the example in Table 32). Palliative coping can become a life pattern, where the only goal is to reduce the inconvenience of intolerable emotions. On the other hand, coping strategies aimed at repairing a damaged relationship naturally also modify the unpleasant emotions in one way or another.

There is great variety in how easy it is to identify palliative strategies in interviews. If the informant has an obvious drug abuse problem, it is easy to interpret this as a kind of escape from their underlying problem(s). But when the subject is penitent due to feelings of guilt, or completely focused on improving their appearance because of shame and guilt, it can be more difficult. The case in Table 32 illustrates this. Clues can be found in the action tendencies of the emotions encountered. At the same time, one should realise that informants are not always willing to talk about their guilt, shame, jealousy, anger and so on – all the unpleasant and socially unacceptable emotions. Such revelations require the subject to trust the researcher; sometimes you have to make your own conclusions about which emotions are present when analysing the interview.

ABSENCE OF COPING: 'PASSIVE RESIGNATION'

Finally, it is necessary to address the possibility that the subject does not take any action in order to improve their situation. More concretely, this means they maintain their expectations in spite of a potentially hopeless situation that causes them distress. This is called *passive resignation* in this analysis, and is accompanied by a so-called narrative of crisis that explains why things are going wrong and why it is impossible to stop them. It is easy to identify those narratives in the interview. They are very often followed by some kind of palliative coping. When the problems cannot be solved, the unpleasant emotions also persist.

Passive resignation can be an expression of one of several different states, and is also typical of the beginning of a crisis and of depressive states. Normally the passivity will be replaced by a more active attitude; if this does not happen for a long period, one ought to consider a pathological state as a possibility, probably depression.

Table 27. Column 5: Interventions

Distressful event	Personal meaning	Emotional implications	Coping strategies	Interventions
1. **Sacked from job**	1.a Loss of relationship with good colleagues	1.a Grief, low spirits, anger	1.a Passive resignation	
	1.b Loss of daily occupation	1.b Grief, sadness	1.b Passive resignation	
	1.c. Loss of social recognition	1.c Shame	1.c Palliative strategy: concealment: does not tell anyone outside the family	
	1.d Loss of authority as the bread winner of the family	1.d Shame, guilt	1.d Palliative strategy: hiding behind the TV (shame), shows penance (guilt): gives more practical help at home. This is also a restoring strategy in relation to 1.b Loss of daily occupation	
	1.e Threat to family's finances the economy of the household.	1.e Fear, anxiety	1.e Attempt to restore the situation: seeking work, reducing costs in the household	1.e.1 Unemployment in society 1.e.2 Spouse has difficulties in saving money
	1.f Threat to marital harmony: the wife is spending too much money	1.f Anger, anxiety, hope	1.f Palliative strategy (anger) and attempt to restore the situation: expressing anger at his wife in hope of making her reduce her spending	1.f.1 The bank forces the sale of the house
	1.g Profit: Freedom from a nasty boss	1.g Relief		

Distressful event	Personal meaning	Emotional implications	Coping strategies	Intervention
2. **House forced on sale**	2.a Loss of home/frame of the family life for a new home	2.a Grief, low spirits, guilt	2.a.1 Passive resignation 2.a.2 Attempt at restoration: looking for a new home for the family	
	2.b Loss of social recognition	2.b Shame	2.b Palliative strategy: does not talk about the situation of the family	
	2.c Loss of harmonious family life	2.c Grief, guilt, anger	2.c.1 Palliative (anger) and attempt with restoration strategy: reproach his wife for lack of solidarity 2.c.2 Palliative strategy (guilt), shows penance: pays more attention to the children, even spoiling them	
3. **Divorce**	3.a Loss of spouse	3.a Grief	3.a Passive resignation	3.a.1 Spouse finds a new partner
	3.b Profit: freedom from the daily disputes with wife	3.b Relief		
	3.c Loss of daily contact with children	3.c Grief, sadness, guilt	3.c.1 Passive resignation 3.c.2 Palliative strategy (guilt), shows penance: spoiling children with sweets and films	
	3.d Loss of daily life with family	3.d Grief, sadness	3.d Passive resignation	
	3.e Loss of satisfaction with life	3.e Depression (this is not a solitary emotion, but a complex clinical state)	3.e Passive resignation: attempt suicide	3.e 1 Relatives take him to a psychiatric ward, where he is diagnosed with depression and receives medical, social, and economic help

Explanation of column 5: Interventions

A coping process can also be brought to an end by external assistance, without any initiative at all from the person in question: this is called intervention (in contrast to coping, where the subject assists themselves).[65] Intervention can come from public institutions, friends, family or others, but may also be completely coincidental, or natural (for instance a spontaneous cure of an illness). It is also important to remember that an intervention can be negative, restricting the subject's ability to cope and even compounding their existing problems. This is seen in the constructed case, Table 27, where the subject's social redirection following the loss of his job, is reinforced by a high rate of unemployment and general economic depression in society. A subject's life circumstances can sometimes limit what they can do to cope.

STEP SIX: Record the outcomes of each sub-process

Table 28. Column 6: Outcomes

In the following the example with the constructed case it will be finished with an analysis of the outcome of the case. This is done when the project is ending.

- *Have new distressing events appeared?* Yes: reduced finances, loss of family home and divorce.
- *Has the event entailed progress as the consequence of the original event?* No progress, apart from being freed from an unpleasant relationship with a manager.
- *Has the person changed their perception of their environment?* Has obtained a more pessimistic view on the world.
- *Did the person change their self-perception?* Reduced self-worth due to all his losses.

- *Did the person (re-)gain wellbeing? (In the scheme this is called both 'mental functioning' and 'mood'. It can also be useful to observe the development of pathology described in the description of the emotions.)* Became depressed, but mood improved after psychiatric treatment.
- *Has the person changed roles? (Role transitions in themselves contain the potential for development, according to Bronfenbrenner, 1979.)* His new roles: unemployed, divorced, single parent.
- *Have the events entailed permanent social changes?* Has developed a closer relationship with his family.
- *Has the event entailed material and economic changes (for example moving home)?* Now lives in a rented flat and pays instalments of the debts. Reduced finances.
- *Has there been permanent reduction or improvement of physical function?* None.
- *Has there been change in daily life?* Living alone, seeing his children every second week, participating in social activities in his new environment.

(Remember: the outcome conclusions are a question of summing up all kinds of resources, progresses and declines of the person.)

In relation to each appraised burden, the outcome of the following coping process should be estimated in order to create a general view of the coping course of the informant. It is important to be sure that all the meanings and emotions in the course are described, in order to investigate which strategies and interventions influence the coping and/or the burdens themselves. Finally, your analysis will provide insight into how very complex, contradictory and filled with dilemmas many coping situations are.

As this is a very detailed work, you must be realistic in terms of how many interviewees to include in a research project. Fewer informants should be preferred, allowing more time for in-depth analyses. The cost of more informants is less time – and perhaps a more superfluous analysis.

STEP SEVEN: Detect patterns across cases

When the detailed analysis of each interview is over, the next step is to compare the cases. Look for patterns that follow the dividing lines in the research population: social groups, types of societal help received, appraisals and types of coping strategies. Are the same events appraised by different people in the same way? How do emotional reactions differ between the groups? Are there any common traits in strategies they use to cope? Lastly, what role do different kinds of intervention play – if any?

Compare the schemes column to column in order to find similarities and differences. There is a clear pattern to be found, for example, in the way sex criminals cope with their stigma (they also agree that they are stigmatised), in that they keep account of who knows about their crime and who does not. This can be seen as pro-active coping, in order to prevent greater condemnation. Similarly, you do not see any active resignation in this group, who experience great losses connected to arrest and sentencing. Almost none can find any positive version of their experience. The closest narrative is: 'It was a good thing that I was stopped' (Munk, in prep). The method is also useful in showing substantial differences within groups that appear homogeneous. For example, I found in a research project about old people's difficulties that the wives of husbands with dementia cope very differently with the task of caring for them (Munk, 1999).

Apart from looking for and finding patterns, the researcher can also look for special narratives. There are four key types:

- The heroic and/or good luck narrative ('How did I avoid the catastrophe?')
- The narrative of resignation ('How can I go on living with this grief?')
- The narrative of crisis ('Why can nothing be done in this situation?')
- The narrative of extinction of value/goal ('Why this is not worth anything to me – and has never been.')

These patterns and narratives, which become visible as a result of the analysis, are central to the presentation of coping research in scientific articles, which is the subject of Chapter 6.

CHAPTER 4

THE COPING INTERVIEW

This chapter concentrates on the interview and the creation of the data that are the object of the analysis. First to be addressed is the relationship between the interviewer and the interviewee. It is a balancing act to encourage the informant to answer the questions fully without feeling used, or offended. Next comes a discussion of the status of the coping interview as a methodology and the reliability of the knowledge gained in the interview, informed by research on self-biographical memory, which is the technical term for the type of knowledge sought in the coping interview. Finally, there is a guide for how to conduct a coping interview and an overview of the typical pitfalls for the coping interviewer.

THE RESEARCH CONTRACT

Attitudes to the interviewee

When you are making an agreement with a potential informant about a research interview, you always make a formal, but also a more informal – perhaps unspoken – contract. These contracts rest on ethical premises that it is the researcher's responsibility to understand and communicate. Apart from the possibility that the interviewee can of course withdraw at any time,[66] you should also make it clear that they participate entirely voluntarily. Conversely, the initiative must always come from the researcher, and the point of departure is the special motives of the researcher. This is the fundamental basis of the contract, which should be built on respect, even in cases where the informants belong to otherwise despised groups such a criminals. Apart from it being bad ethics, a lack of respect will produce more or less useless research, as the informant is unlikely to reveal their true feelings to a disrespectful interviewer. It is also vital to distinguish the research contract from a therapeutic one; it is not for the researcher to treat the informant. As a teacher I have sometimes heard students express the opinion that the researcher should be provocative in a coping interview. This is a fundamental misunderstanding (see *The pitfalls of the research interview* in the last part of this chapter).

The distribution of roles

There should be no doubt about the distribution of roles between the interviewee and the interviewer. It is the interviewer who establishes the theme of the interview and also directs it. When the contract about the interview is being made, it is important to agree what the dialogue is going to be about, so that the interviewer has obtained the right to ask the relevant questions. If the interviewer begins to suspect that the interview is going in the wrong direction, they have the right to ask if the information being provided is relevant to the theme of the interview. One has to be careful here, however, because you can never be sure that what you might think is irrelevant is in fact irrelevant. There is always the possibility that you cannot see it as an outsider, and you cannot guess what is coming. A question about relevance can make you appear impatient, and give the impression that you are using the interviewee for your own ends without having any personal interest in them. Of course, there is some truth in this; your relationship was established because you are running a research project and need informants. A balance must be found, and it is good to make oneself clear at the outset, so that you can work purposefully to avoid the interviewee feeling exploited.

Finally, you also have to explain that there will often be differences in status between the researcher and the interviewee. In order to improve the quality of the interview the researcher must recognise that this influences the dynamics of the interview deeply. The task is to minimize the consequences. Most often the researcher will be perceived as having the higher status, but the opposite may also be seen. If the researcher formally has the highest status, a humble attitude is appropriate. On the other hand, if the interviewee has high status, it is necessary for the interviewer not to seemed cowed, in order to have some influence on the interview and to avoid being unquestioningly uncritical. We are often unconscious of these dynamics.

Another aspect of the contract is that the interviewer must be able to understand what they are being told by the interviewee. This means they should be allowed to ask for more explanation and clarification using summaries in their own words ('Should what you are saying be understood in this or that way?', or 'It sounds as if you mean this? Is that true?'). This increases the validity of the results, because the final interpretation of what is said can be controlled by the interviewee. However, the researcher should not count on always agreeing with the informant about their interpretations of their reactions and standpoints. Sometimes, you will find a contrast between what is said and the emotions expressed. The informant should of course be told that you see this contrast; this will sometimes result in a modification of their statements – and sometimes not. Under all circumstances it is wise to try to reduce or prevent conflict about this. Disagreement on a single statement is not enough to spoil a whole research project, but it should still be excluded from the analysis. Another solution is simply to describe what you see and leave the interpretation to the reader. In other words, we have an ethical dilemma here because the researcher does not have the right to put their own interpretation in print without the consent of the interviewee.[67]

The art of the researcher is in not exercising their the right to direct the interview too insistently. You must always remember that the interviewee is the one who knows best about their experiences. It is therefore a good idea to emphasise to the informant before the interview that it is not about performing, and there is no 'right' or 'wrong'. It is the informant who is the expert here.

For the interview to be successful, it should run as an engaged conversation where both parties are interested in understanding the life situation of the informant and in solving puzzles. When informants have agreed to participate, and the researcher has a kind, respectful and engaged attitude, there almost are no limits to the kinds of questions you can ask, if they are relevant to the topic you have agreed to discuss.

Informants have many different reasons for participating in research. Some are motivated by the idea that others (perhaps even persons with a perceived high status) are interested in one's – in own eyes – quite average life.[68] Perhaps an informant wants to help others who have the same problems as them, or perhaps they feel guilt and shame about their actions and want make amends somehow, and to improve both their self-perception and their public image. In other words, as an interviewer you may be a tool in your informant's coping process without knowing it.

Practical arrangements

Before the research contract is made with the informant, the researcher should provide them with all the relevant information so that they can contemplate it, and return to it if something creates some doubt (Thisted, 2018). The document should say:

- What the interview is about;
- That the participant can withdraw from the interview at any time;
- That there is full anonymity;
- That the interview will be taped; and
- How much time – on average – the interview will take.

Conclusion

In one of the first phases of a coping research project the researcher must make a formal (and in some ways also informal) contract
with potential informants. The contract is primarily about
the ethical rules by which the researhcer is bound and the distribution of roles between the researcher and the informant. It is
crucial that the interviewer/researcher is aware of both.

COPING MEMORIES: STORED, FORGOTTEN OR CHANGED?

The memory process and self-biographical memories

When people are interviewed about their own lives, one has to
realise that it is not possible to obtain a direct report. Since the
informant is recalling something from their memory, you are
only getting the stored memory representations of the events
(Thomsen, 2006; Thomsen & Brinkmann, 2009). Consulting
research on memory will thus help you establish a firmer foundation of knowledge for your project, by better understanding:

- The memory processes in general;
- The reliability of self-biographical memories
  – especially of upsetting events;
- The nature of forgetting; and
- The consequences of all these for the interview.

Types of knowledge

Before we take a closer look at memory processes as such, it
should be mentioned that memory research differentiates between three types of knowledge, each with different characteristics (Eysenck & Keane, 2005):

- Self-biographic/episodic knowledge
- Semantic/general knowledge
- Procedural knowledge

Self-biographical knowledge is structured by subjects; it is chronological and contextual, that is, organised in the memory in relation to time and place in the person's life. Self-biographical knowledge is structured as continual narrative that is reorganised and built on throughout the life course, in parallel with new experiences and reflections on what happened (See f.ex. Cohler, 1982; McAdams, 2001). This does not mean that we are not able to keep track of the before and after, because we are also able to remember how our attitudes to our experiences changed.

Semantic knowledge, on the contrary, is separated from time and place in the way it is organised in the memory. Of course, it is still connected to concrete practices in concrete periods of time – as for example historical information about Ancient Greece. But when this knowledge becomes general knowledge, for instance in a textbook, it is stored apart from memories of one's personal life. Knowledge about Ancient Greece can, of course, be a part of a personal life, for instance memories of learning about the subject at school. But the subject itself will very likely primarily be stored outside of this context, in a category such as 'history' or 'the antique world'.[69]

These two forms of knowledge, semantic and self-biographical, are both accessible in language. This is not the case for the last form of knowledge, *procedural knowledge*, which entails physical processes and patterns of action. Typical examples are patterns of actions in the practical world such as riding a bike or lacing shoes. This also counts for all routines associated with the professional practice of the person.[70] It is the type of knowledge which is the most robust when people are suffering from memory loss, for example in relation to Alzheimer's disease, probably because it is created over many years of repetition.[71] Patients with Alzheimer's who can no longer speak may still remember how to carry out activities and procedures they learnt earlier in their lives.

The phases of the memory process

In these discussions about the memory process, it is exclusively self-biographical knowledge we are considering (though many of the points are also relevant to other types), since that is the focus of the manual.

In general, it can be said that memories are dynamic and sometimes quite complex to understand. Briefly, cognitive science differentiates between three phases of the memory process, which are more or less intentional (Eysenck & Keane, 2005; Thomsen, 2006):

- Selecting the information
- Storing the 'selected' information
- Searching in the memory store: recognition and recall

1. Selecting information

First, information is selected for storing.[72] Since we do not have the capacity to overview and store all the stimuli we experience, it is necessary to differentiate between these and to organise the selected information as appropriately and economically as possible. The following criteria of selection seem to be general (Eysenck & Keane, 2005; Thomsen, 2006):

- Personal relevance
- Atypicality
- Newness

2. Storing the 'selected' information

A striking analogy of the storing process is the arranging of books in a library so that it is possible to find them again. Information is selected according to personal criteria of relevance, then stored according to categories, as in library catalogues. Active searching in the memory, known as *recall*, is done with prompts that mirror these categories, as in a library. But the library metaphor has its limitations regarding memories of one's own life. These are stored according not only to categories, but also to chronology and the contexts in which the experience happened. This means that there are more cues for recalling these memories than there are for nonpersonal subject categories. These cues are also more often related to more sensory modalities (sight, sound, smell, taste, touch) of concrete contexts, which makes for better storage of the information. The library metaphor still stands in that these cues can be a help in finding the subject you are looking for. The storing – and also the recall – is multidimensional:

- *Across*: the cues are affiliated to the contextual frame for the process of storing (sight, smell, sound, etc.)
- *Along:* the information is organised on an axis of time

Apart from the categorising cues, two other aspects are especially important in relation to successful storage of memories, namely repetition and depth. Robust memories are integrated into a network of multi-modal associations, and are therefore more moving and specific (Eysenck & Keane, 2005; Draaisma, 2006). This rich network of associations also makes recall easier.

In recent years research has shown that the reliability of memories can be a tricky matter. They can undergo continuous reinterpretations, and people even have memories of things that never happened, which they trust deeply (Mazzoni, Loftus & Kirsch, 2001; Loftus, 2003; Loftus & Davis, 2006).

In terms of normal memory function, we assume that essential events in one's life will *always* be stored, and that they will not be manipulated as self-biographical material (Eysenck & Keane, 2005). Personal experiences can have very different degrees of personal relevance, and it seems that the degree of relevance is crucial to the reliability of memories. Events of greater personal relevance – that is, ones that are intensely emotional due to losses or achievements of personal goals – are easier to date than events of minor personal relevance; high personal relevance strengthens the reliability of memories (Conway & Pleydell-Pearce, 2000).

Another type of memory that seems more immune to forgetting or reconstruction involves atypical events that are not necessarily related to one's personal life. Such memories evade the phenomenon of interference. The result is that repeated events of the same kind, such as going to school every day, will be stored in the same category, eventually merging and becoming impossible to differentiate. They will be remembered as 'the typical school day'. In contrast, when something unusual or surprising happens it is remembered more specifically (Thomsen, 2006). Finally, the value of *newnesss* also means something for the strength of a memory, for much the same reasons.

According to the American psychologist and memory researcher David Pillemer, who has worked on self-biographical memory over the life course, the *function* of specific memories also plays a role in their robustness (in Thomsen, 2006: 87). Here we will only focus on the function the memories have for the self, because these seem to be especially important for the coping analysis. Following the Danish cognitive psychologist Dorthe Thomsen (2006), Pillemer defines three categories of memories with self-functions:

1. Events which define the beginning of the life trajectory of the self;
2. Turning points which suddenly change one's life course;
3. Events which have a fundamental meaning that anchors certain values and ideas of life.

A fourth category was added by Robinson (1992) and Thomsen & Berntsen (2005):

4. Events which entail progress or hindrances regarding goals.[73]

This is another way of describing the selection criteria mentioned above: *personal relevance, atypicality* and *newness*. The difference here is that they are all connected with the self, a connection that is also made in the concept of *personal relevance*. According to Thomsen (2006), these events have a defining influence on the structure of the narrative of the self, creating a chronological chain of causes that constitutes one's self-understanding.

Today, the common idea that suppressed traumatic memories can be recalled from the subconscious in psychotherapy after having been forgotten in many years is rejected by current memory research. On the contrary, it seems that especially traumatic events can never be forgotten (Loftus & Davis, 2006). The question of so-called 'restored memories' is often about sexual abuse in childhood. In these cases, it seems that such 'memories' are created by the suggestive influence of a therapist (Mazzoni, Loftus & Kirsch, 2001; Loftus, 2003; Loftus & Davis, 2006). Memories of events that inspire shame unfortunately seem to be indelible (Draaisma, 2006). Shameful memories, for example of personal failure, rarely surface in the positive self-narratives the interviewer most often hears. They have not been forgotten, but censored by the interviewee. In other words, there are some indications that exactly the types of memories we are seeking in the coping interview are especially resilient to forgetting and manipulations. This is because they are about events that were crucial to important goals and often traumatic, and thus also atypical. Finally, existential difficulties tend to last a long time, and this, in combination with the emotional influence, results in a lot of reflection on the situation. Repetition and reflection improve the storing process. The special problem with self-censorship is difficult to handle as a researcher; you can only pay attention to it (see below for a discussion of pitfalls in the interview).

3. Searching in the memory store: recognition and recall

Technically there are two kinds of search process: 'recognition' and 'recall'. The first process is very simple, and the second quite complicated.

Recognition is a simple and to a certain extent passive process. All that is retrieved is a copy of the stored information, and no active search or cues are needed (Eysenck & Keane, 2005). This process is not relevant for the coping interview.

Recall, on the other hand, is understood as an active process of searching in which the person needs a cue in order to find the information of interest. It is very much like looking for a needle in a haystack; if you do not have any cues at all you will not find anything. The consequence is that you do not know where to begin or end.

To the informant, the interview is just such a process of recall. It cannot be expected that the informant will find the required information in a short time if they are not prepared for the questions, or if the questions are too unspecific. It is commonly assumed that the informant should be surprised by the questions, with no opportunity to prepare for them, so that they have no opportunity to manipulate the information. On the contrary, however, a lack of preparation time actually reduces the reliability of the interview.

Forgetting

It is not obvious which information will be stored and which not. This fact can have quite serious consequences, for instance in connection with witness evidence in criminal trials (Loftus, 2003). There are several reasons why information may be difficult to find:

- It may never have been stored at all
- The person may not have the right cue to find the information

- The information may have been confused with other, similar information (the aforementioned problem of interference)
- The information may be so peripheral that it has eroded away due to unprecise storing and/or lack of repetition (Eysenck & Keane, 2005)

Finally, it should be emphasised that special conditions, such as mental illness and the side effects of pharmaceuticals, can reduce the ability to recall or construct reliable and detailed memories from the memory store.

A model for autobiographical memory

In a coping interview, you want interviewee to recall reliable memories about a specific, personally relevant period in their lives, perhaps from many years ago. Ideally, this includes the chain of events, how the person interpreted them and acted at the time, and what was happening in their surroundings. Such memories will certainly be associated with strong feelings for the interviewee.

The British memory researchers Conway and Pleydell-Pearce (2000) suggest a model for what they call the 'self-memory' system, an organised structure for a knowledge base that includes self-biographical memories. This concept is very close to what we normally call the 'self'. The ability to store information about one's own life is fundamental for the understanding of the self in its many facets (experience, learning, identity, social behaviour and so on). In association with this 'self-memory' system human beings also have a so-called 'working memory' (previously known as 'short-term memory'), which Conwell and Pleydell-Pearce (ibid.) call the 'working self'. This covers the cognitive activities that happen as the recollections are constructed, starting with the 'self-memory' system, a kind of database of the self. 'Constructing' here means that the working self is locating material from the self-memory store, and translating it into language in order to share it with others. This adds complexity to the problem of having enough good cues, which is treated in the section below.

Memory researchers agree to a large extent that recollections are created against the background of the goal structures or goal hierarchy of the subject, and that they are to a large extent related to the realisation or loss of personal goals. Consequently, it is the 'working self' we are interviewing about coping processes, or for that matter any other aspects of the life of the person. In self-biographical memory research, it has been shown that there are three levels of recollections associated with the self (Conway & Pleydell-Pearce, 2000). These levels are integrated into each other and should not be thought of as a rigid 'layer cake'.

The three levels can be useful for the interviewer. An array of open questions starting with *when, what, where, how* and *which* can stimulate the construction of relevant recollections from the memory store, since they involve the dimensions (time and context) in which the cues are stored. The levels are:

1. *Periods in life with time as the organising principle*, which are integrated into the timeline of the life course and consequently chronological in structure. A period has a beginning, a middle and an end. The boundaries of a life period are not necessarily sharp, and they may be stored thematically or according to transitions that happened at specific, well-defined times. In a life course there will also be many kinds of parallel and overlapping periods that are connected with environments.

In order to support the informant in recollecting the events stored on this level, you ask *when*, and it can be useful to keep track of a chronological structure in the interview. The structure of the storage process is chronological, and the chronology will function as a cue for the informant in the questions you ask ('What happened then?', 'And after that?').

2. *General events connected to the realisation/loss of goals*, which entail single events, repeated events and sequences of events. One example might be the death of a spouse, where the spouse is the lost goal. These recollections are more specific and take the form of small stories about a coping course, as well as relevant knowledge for the self, for example the fulfilment or loss of goals. Here the organising principle is not the time dimension, but the fate of personal goals. The relevant questions are *what* happened in relation to the goals of the informant and *which* reactions, reflections and actions were released in the person and their environment.

3. *Event-specific concrete knowledge*, which is more detailed and accompanied by concrete images. One example might be the moment someone finds out they have a fatal illness. If the event was dramatic and unusual they are often remembered in 'flash bulb memories', in which small details about the situation are frozen in the memory and may be recollected vividly even after many years. Here the questions are primarily *what*, *how*, and *who*.

Guidance from memory research for the interviewer

On the background of fairly recent memory research, Thomsen and Brinkmann (2009: 306–308) provide much good advice for the interviewer to help them optimise their reports of specific recollections:

1. *Give the informant time to recall* and emphasise that it is normal for it to take some time. Recall is a hierarchic search, where material is recalled and then translated.

2. *Give the informant concrete cues* to help them in their search. It is important to give cues that are relevant to the way the material is stored in the 'knowledge bank'

of the brain. If your cues are off, you risk the informant giving a negative answer even when they have experienced the thing you are seeking. This may happen not only when the experience not stored under the cue you give, but also when your cue it too abstract and diffuse. The solution is to be more concrete in your questions.

3. *Use typical categories of specific recollections in order to find useful cues*, preparing your questions based on concrete categories. Questions that require informants to give an overview of many experiences across contexts and time will result in vague and abstract answers. As for the coping interview, it is my experience that asking about distressing events when the informant has had time to think about their answers in advance is the best way.

4. *Ask for more specific recollections from a more recent period*, since investigations of specific recollections show a consistent recency effect, with more details being remembered.

5. *Use a relevant timeline*, giving remarkable events as contextual cues in order to help the recall of older events. This is particularly useful if you want to know about events from a long time ago in the person's life. Be precise about the period you are interested in (e.g. 'When you were at high school...'); if it is possible to identify unusual events from the period this will help the informant to recall the material.

6. *Ask the informant to speak freely and expansively about the specific recollection*, since in witness research it is shown that free, detailed narratives produce reliable recall (Thomsen & Brinkmann, 2009).

The seductive storyteller

Recollections can have several functions in social situations, and a research interview is no exception. Listening to a story told in a lively, even spellbinding manner can easily lead the interviewer to forget to ask questions. Stories have direction; they involve many emotions; they can be rich with diverse sensory details. For all these reasons, you might forget to ask critical questions concerning the reliability of what you are told (Thomsen, 2006). In other words, narratives are seductive. It is wise, therefore, to realise that a story told by an informant in an interview consists of more layers:

- A description of a sequence
- An interpretation of the sequence
- A layer of self-construction (in order to present a socially respectable image of oneself)

Apart from the fact that memory research can reassure us that the coping interview will produce reliable material, you should also operate with two criteria in relation to the question of reliability:

1. Does the story sound realistic?
2. Is the story consistent? Here the model of the coping analysis can help the researcher to investigate whether the story is psychologically coherent.

Conclusion

According to memory research, it seems that the type of recollections we are looking for in the coping interview are especially robust in terms of forgetting or interference from other kinds of recollections. This is reassuring from the point of view of the researcher; better storage means greater probability of reliable recall. However, you should also be aware that an informant's recollections may be so fascinatingly told that you forget to ask the questions that are of interest in the project. Recollections of this character are not vulnerable to forgetting, but they may sometimes and to some extent be reconstructed during their time as memories. Interesting and/or traumatic recollections are regularly recalled silently and/or explicitly, and are thus exposed to small twists of new understandings and interpretations. This can be a kind of figure–ground process, where some aspects are accentuated more than others. Recent research in self-biographical memory gives good advice to help the researcher obtain more reliable recollections from informants.

THE COPING INTERVIEW AS A NON-LINEAR PROCESS

It is now clear that the interview should be understood as a process of recall, is defined as an active, voluntary and conscious search in one's memory with the help of cues. The 'working self' creates search models using cues to facilitate recall of relevant information in the memory store. One should appreciate that no interview can follow a clear chronology where all the recollections attached to one event appear at once, even if the process of storing is chronological. Like the following analysis, the interview is both a progressive process and a *recursive* one, where you will need to return to matters discussed earlier in order to discover more aspects as they appear during the process of recall, because this process creates new cues. Once the process has begun there will very likely be 'involuntary' recollections, which again create new cues for recall. These involuntary recollections are not necessarily of unpleasant events, but of events that were not actively sought. They may very well be relevant for the interview, and it seems that these kinds of recollections may never be recalled voluntarily – hence the label 'involuntary' (Eysenck & Keane, 2005). The best strategy is thus to let the interview run as a conversation, without asking irrelevant questions, because this breaks up both the conversation and the recall process. During natural pauses in the conversation, the interviewer can return to issues treated earlier in order to obtain more detail and also to be sure that they have understood what has been said (Kvale, 1989).

The researcher must of course be aware of the purpose of the interview, but with some training they can learn both to show spontaneity, in the shape of new ideas that are relevant to the reflective and narrative process, *and* to exercise superior control. Since the topic of the interview has been agreed beforehand, it is also easier to get the conversation back on track.

The researcher must recognise that interviews always appear messy and disconnected at the time because recollections do not emerge logically and evenly. This also counts for the transcription. Afterwards, during the analysis, you can order both chronology and causality in the coping course.

Conclusion

The coping interview should be considered as a process of recollection and reflection, and the researcher should not interfere with too many questions, which can disturb these processes. Do not imagine the interview as a linear process; the overview will come during the ensuing analysis.

INTERVIEW GUIDE FOR THE COPING PROCESS

It is important that the researcher *does not* use technical, academic terms during the interview or expect that the interviewee should be able to do so. The interview should take place using a common language of everyday life. It is the responsibility of the researcher to interpret what is said from the perspective of the conceptual analytic frame. It can be tempting to try to impose technical analytical terms on the interviewee, especially if you yourself are insecure about using these terms. But when you are experienced in the technique, you will be able tacitly to translate the everyday language used by the interviewee into these concepts during the interview. This requires confidence with the concepts and the whole idea behind the coping analysis, which is not to say that you cannot do an interview before you have achieved this. Carry out your first interviews with the help of the following interview guide, and then you will find you learn as you go along. If you lose courage during the first interviews, you can comfort yourself with the fact that even beginners' interviews almost always contain useful material! The guide mirrors the analytic coping process. The open questions in the review of the analytic model can be used along with the interview process, if it seems relevant.

Interview guide

A: Distressing event(s)	'Can you tell me what caused these problems for you?'
B: Personal meaning	'What negative things happened for you personally because of this?' 'Have you had any losses?' 'Is there anything that you cannot do any more?' 'Have there been any positive consequences?'
C: Emotional implications	'What did you feel about what happened?'
D: Coping strategies	'What did you do then?' (coping question) 'What did you do to help you endure the situation?' (palliative question)
E: Intervention	'Did anyone help you?' (initiative from other people) 'What else happened?' (other influences)
F: Outcome(s)	'How did it end?' 'Was the problem solved?' 'Have there been permanent changes in your life?' 'If so, what kind of changes?' 'Is there anything that you have changed your mind about?' 'Yourself?' 'Your life?' 'Your environment?' 'How is your wellbeing?' 'Have any of your roles changed?' 'Were there other changes: social, material, financial, physical or in your everyday life?'

Further comments on the interview

A: Distressing event(s)

Here the interviewee labels the events that caused problems for them during the period of time delineated by the researcher. In general, the answers will be in the present or past tense, depending on whether the process is over or not.

B: Personal meaning

Here the important point is to get hold of the *meaning* the event had for the informant. Remember the simple categories of *threats*, *losses*, *challenges* and/or *profit*. The answers to these questions could for example be:

- 'I do not see my daughter any more' (The 'translation' to the terms of the analytic scheme could be: 'Loss of contact with a loved one')
- 'I can no longer walk' (Translation: 'Loss of mobility and autonomy; loss of identity as a healthy person')
- 'I have lost my job' (Translation: 'Loss of earning opportunity, recognition and identity as a worker')
- 'I found a tumour in my breast, and the doctor told me it was cancer' (Translation: 'Threat of death' – though note this answer is closer to those found at step A above)

C: Emotional implications

Here the interviewer has to be conscious about the whole register of emotions. Gradually one will learn to find out which emotions have been or are part of the reaction to the distressful event on the background of the core relational theme which is in each emotion. If the meaning is described then you have to look for the emotion and vice versa.

D: Coping strategies

How was the damage met or repaired? Was there any palliation of the aversive emotions? Remember to avoid the technical coping expressions. Listen to the narratives of the course.

E: Interventions

Did anyone help you, or did you meet more barriers?

F: Outcome(s)

Be conscious about the two types of narratives of resignation, and of burdening emotions, which can become permanent, manifesting in guilt, shame, anger/bitterness, grief, fright, anxiety and so on. See the descriptions of pathology in the section about emotions above.

THE PITFALLS OF THE RESEARCH INTERVIEW

This chapter concludes with an overview of potential pitfalls of the coping interview. As mentioned earlier, a good research interview is in many ways similar to an engaged conversation, where the researcher and the interviewee are both occupied in studying aspects of the issues in question. The difference is the asymmetry between the two people: the researcher has been given the power to direct the conversation, which focuses solely on the life of the interviewee. The following pitfalls, some of which have been mentioned before, can prevent the researcher obtaining suitable, relevant information, and also make the interview less reliable:

- *Too many questions.* The conversation is broken up, preventing conversational flow, which is crucial to a successful interview.
- *Questions put in an overly specific, rigid order.* Again preventing conversational flow, this will markedly reduce the

quality of the interview. It is still possible to get answers to your questions even if they are not put in a certain order. Furthermore, improvisation in relation to unexpected matters is made more difficult.

- *The interviewee has too little time to recollect.* It takes some time for the interviewee to recall relevant memories; without sufficient time, the reliability of their answers will be reduced.
- *The interviewee directs the interview.* The researcher may miss some important questions, and/or will fail to take the interview in the planned direction. (This happens most commonly when the interviewed person has a higher social status than the researcher).
- *The interviewer is too humble.* The informant is not challenged enough, and the interviewer does not question the arguments behind the interviewee's statements. In the worst cases, the researcher forms a bond with the interviewee and thus relinquishes their neutrality – or, conversely, they become anxious or even afraid of the interviewee (most commonly in so-called 'expert' interviews).
- *The researcher knows the interview person too well.* In such cases too much becomes implicit, and there may be delicate questions the researcher does not dare ask.
- *The interviewer mistreats the interviewee.* Even if the informant has given their consent to the interview and is thoroughly informed about its purpose, they may not want to participate fully. This may happen if the interview touches on particularly painful memories, or ones that make them feel ashamed or disloyal to family or friends. Even if the body language of the informant shows their discomfort, the interviewer can sometimes be insensible to it and continue to ask difficult questions. When the personal boundaries of the informant are not respected, this will have consequences for the entire interview.

- *The interviewer asks vague and abstract questions.* This can make it difficult for the informant to understand what the researcher wants to know. The risk is that their answers will also be vague and abstract. Another risk is that the informant answers on the basis of non-representative, specific events, leading to unreliable generalisations (Thomsen & Brinkmann, 2009). If you have any doubt, ask a more concrete question.
- *The interviewer uses words that the informant does not understand.* Often informants will not say when they do not understand, meaning the interviewer and interviewee will continue to talk at cross-purposes. This also reduces the reliability of the interview.
- *The interviewer asks only 'closed' questions.* This restricts the interviewee's involvement and reflection.
- *The interviewer praises the informant repeatedly when they answer.* Too much flattery can appear patronising, and may also bias the information the interviewee gives. This is especially pronounced in interviews with patients, children and old people.
- *The interviewer asks leading questions.* There is an assumption that such questions will provoke the informant to express the truth more vehemently. On the contrary, the risk is that they give a biased version of the history in which you are interested (Loftus, 2007).

CHAPTER 5

THE LIFE-HISTORICAL RESOURCE INTERVIEW

This chapter can be regarded as a supplement to the coping analysis. The life-historical resource interview is not a necessary prerequisite, but it does add an interesting – and informative – dimension to the analysis. It does not matter whether you do it before or after the coping analysis. Chapter 2 states that resources of many kinds can play a crucial role coping with problems, and preventing them. A person's access to resources also affects the outcome of the experience. It was emphasised that the concept of resource covers everything from personality traits to genetics to finances.

In a coping interview, we explore the resources available to the person in the present. But this does not give us any understanding of the history behind those resources, or the background against which the person is acting. The primary aspect here is personal resources, but also the positive and negative interplay with society and dominant cultural values. Following the trajectory of the interviewee's life, with all its opportunities and constraints, will allow for a deeper understanding of the coping situation you are interested in. For a developmental psychologist, like this author, the question will be about positive and negative reinforcement in the person's life. Even if you cannot deduce the origins of a certain reaction, the life-historical resource interview will give you a better understanding of why people react very differently to the same kinds of life events.

The structure of a life-historical resource interview

It seems logical to construct a life-historical interview around transitions in life, which correspond with shifts in roles. Changes in social position in themselves have the potential for changes in life (Bronfenbrenner, 1979). In modern life, there exists an array of parallel systems producing transitions. A well-known example is the path through the educational system and through work life; another obvious example is the family system and the appearance and disappearance of members by birth, death, marriage/new partners and divorce. But the overall system of society – of the state and civil society – also creates unexpected transitions in connection with larger societal changes such as economic depression, wars or epidemics, for example, which can radically change a person's life circumstances. These transitions have the potential for personal development, giving access to new resources, but also carry risks, or indeed a combination of both. But even when there have not been such unexpected changes in society, it is important to obtain information in the interview about the historical period in which the informant was born, as this will help you understand the opportunities and challenges the informant has experienced.

During the investigation of a life course you will work chrono-logically, asking about where the person was born and in what sort of emotional and financial environment; what their parents did for a living; what their ethnic background was; what the fundamental values of the family were; and whether they were healthy as a child.

When pursuing an informant's life history, it is a good idea to focus on the following fields of resources, on transitions, and on the choices taken voluntarily or involuntarily:

- Education
- Public help
- Addition or disappearance of material resources
- Addition or disappearance of social resources (friends and family)
- Development of personal values
- Development of sources of joy
- Development of personality: the balance between resignation, action, and decisiveness
- Development of personality: self-worth, self-confidence, forward planning, sociability

In discussing these issues in the interview, you will obtain a fairly coherent picture of local contributory connections in the life of the interviewee.

Analytic scheme for resources

To analyse the information you have obtained regarding resources, make a scheme like that shown in Table 29. Decide for yourself how detailed the descriptions should be in each column. At the top, record the interviewee's gender, age (at the time of the interview), ethnic background, historical period of childhood and adolescence, childhood environment and material conditions. This comprises a description of the outset of the life trajectory of the interviewee.

Table 29.
Year of birth, gender, ethnic background, values, historical period of childhood, childhood environment and material conditions.

Role transitions	Public help	Material resources	Social resources	Health	Sources of joy	Personal values	Resignation/ activity/ decisiveness	Self-confidence

When the life course is analysed and the role transitions are written into the scheme, you have a reasonable point of departure for comparative studies of the different backgrounds of individuals and groups, their life trajectories and their methods of coping with distressing events. In combination with the coping analysis this information can provide the background for a separate scientific qualitative article.

CHAPTER 6

PUBLICATION OF THE RESULTS OF THE MICROANALYSIS

In this chapter I will explain how to present your analyses in the form of schemes and narratives in scientific articles. The problem of how to present qualitative research is a recurring one; mostly, quotations are used, and while this is a possibility for the coping analyses, schematic summaries and narratives give a better overview. It is also possible to use all three elements separately or together in an article.

SCHEMES OF RESULTS REGARDING COPING COURSES

Comparisons of similarities and differences in a group can also be put in schemes; descriptions of typical and atypical solitary courses may also be of interest in an article. Whether you are presenting comparisons, patterns or an atypical course, you should use the analytic categories of the scheme as your tools of comparison. These categories also allow for an overview, so that results may be presented in a more condensed form than is seen in the common and sometimes very extensive articles using quotations. In Table 30 examples are shown of a presentation of a homogenic pattern in a larger group, and Table 31 shows a coping course for a single person.

The first example is a scheme of results on a coping analysis of 19 convicted child abusers and their way of coping with their stigma as 'paedophile criminals'. Homogenic patterns are seen in the different analytic categories. In spite of other kinds of differences in the group (see 'Examples of coping narratives'), the interpretations, reactions and actions in relation to their conviction are remarkably similar. The results in the following table cover most of the 19 men. The differences are noted in the scheme.

Table 30. Presentation of a homogenic pattern of behaviour in a larger group

Coping analysis of convicted child sex abusers

Personal meaning	• Loss of recognition • Loss of a 'clean' CV • Loss of friends and colleagues (sometimes also a spouse) • Loss of work • Loss of a personal finances • Threat of persecution in daily life • Threat of disclosure to persons who do not know the verdict, for example by the police and the media • Threats about loss of recognition among people who do not know the story
Emotional implications	• Anxiety • Fear • Shame • Guilt • Grief • Anger
Coping strategies	*Attempts to prevent any aggravation* • Keeping account of who knows and who does not • Staying silent about conviction and prison experience • Creating false criminal identity to explain why they are in prison to other prisoners and to others who know about their imprisonment *Palliative strategies* • Periodical displacement of threats and accompanying misery *Passive resignation* • Yes. Frustration since there are few options for improving their situation. Decreases over time.

Interventions	*Positive:* • Parents and siblings give help and support, sometimes also spouses or new girlfriends who know about the crime. • Offers of treatment from society, which also mitigates the conviction as it also implies a kind of 'sickness' and lack of responsibility *Negative:* • Persecution because of detection of criminal identity
Outcome(s)	• The distressing situation never completely ends (one participant commits suicide) • New burdens: social rejection • Progress: yes, one participant is cured from alcohol addiction; more find new, empathetic partners • Developmental changes: more differentiated (meaning positive) view of stigmatised groups in society; more critical view of the justice system; changed view of children (they are 'dangerous') • Wellbeing: gradually regained; most of the men find new understanding girlfriends (who all know about the convictions) • Role changes: stigmatised as criminal (the majority reject the label 'paedophile'); have a double identity for the rest of their lives • Social changes: permanent loss of friends; new girlfriends; continue their existence in a more or less marginalised social position • Material changes: moving to another location where nobody knows about them • Economical changes: reduced personal finances (all) • Changes in everyday life: continuous threat that people will find out about their crimes

There is no example here of how to communicate the life-historical resource interview, but a matrix system (Miles & Huberman, 1994) will give you a quick overview on the social background of your group of informants. A matrix of the social backgrounds of the sex criminals presented in the scheme above would show life histories with several forms of marginalisation and lacking many kinds of resources.

The next example is a presentation of the coping course of an 80-year-old woman whose whole story is given in the appendix. This case reveals how this generation of women fulfilled the roles expected of them in the historical period, even if they felt no personal inclination towards them. The case is complex; it is filled with dilemmas and contradictions that have to be captured by a coping analysis. This case illustrates a timeline of the coping course. The numbers in the table refer to the implications of each distressing event in chronological order. Notice how a strategy can have several aims or objectives.

Table 31. Presentation of an individual course

Coping analysis of a woman caring for a husband with dementia

Distressing events	1. Spouse suffering from dementia 2. Spouse is moved to a nursing home as a part-time inhabitant by initiative of the wife 3. Spouse is later moved to a nursing home as a permanent full-time inhabitant by initiative of the wife 4. Personal reaction to death of spouse
Personal meaning	1. *Challenge* to live up to the moral imperative to look after one's spouse 1. *Loss* of personal freedom 2. and 3. *Loss* of self-image as a dutiful wife 2. and 3. *Profit:* more freedom than she has ever experienced in her adult life 4. *Profit from death of the spouse:* Total freedom from duties towards spouse 4. *Loss of* self-image as a decent human being (It is against any moral rule to be happy and relieved about another person's death)
Emotions	1. *Hope:* That she will live up to the challenge; a dilemma between duty and implications for her freedom 1. *Anger/irritation:* Due to loss of personal freedom 2. and 3. *Guilt:* Could not live up to the personal moral imperative 2. and 3. *Anger against the self:* Could not live up to the personal moral imperative

2. and 3. *Shame:* Could not live up to the image of being a 'dutiful wife'

2. and 3. *Relief:* Achieves freedom

4. *Guilt:* 'One does not feel relief over the death of others!'; breaks another moral rule

Coping strategies	1. *Prevention in order to meet the challenge/attempt to restore personal freedom:* Looking after spouse every hour of every day
	1. Arranges part-time care at a nursing home; takes a holiday
	1. Moves spouse permanently to a nursing home on own initiative
	2., 3. and 4. *Attempt to restore the reduced image:*
	– Furnishes the spouse's room at the nursing home nicely
	– Visits spouse every day and sends postcards when she is away on holiday
	– Tells her GP and her children what she has done
	– Conceals her relief over the death of spouse
	Palliative strategies
	1. *Soothes her anger and irritation* by taking the initiative to move spouse to a nursing home as a part-time patient; no longer full-time carer of spouse
	1. *Soothes her anger and irritation* by taking the initiative to move spouse permanently to a nursing home; no longer carer of spouse at all
	1. *Attempt to soothe her shame* by furnishing spouse's room at the nursing home nicely, visiting him daily and sending postcards when she is on holiday
	3. *Attempt to soothe her guilt* by furnishing spouse's room at the nursing home nicely, visiting him daily and sending postcards when she is on holiday. 'Penance' in technical terms
	Passive resignation
	1. Frustrated over loss of freedom
	2. and 3. Gives up on the challenge to care for spouse
	4. Frustration over feeling relief about death of spouse
Positive intervention	2. and 3. The manager of the nursing home asks her not to come in on Saturday afternoons because her husband enjoys watching football games on television at that time (soothes her guilt and shame); in general he enjoys the nursing home
	4. Spouse has a stroke and dies shortly after (intervention from 'nature')

Outcome	(The wife moves spouse permanently to a nursing home on own initiative)
	End of battle to meet the challenge releases:
	• *A new dilemma:* permanent emotion of guilt regarding husband; permanent emotion of shame regarding social environment; reduced self-worth
	• *Wellbeing:* relief and better mood, freedom partly achieved
	• *Changes of role:* no longer primary caregiver of spouse
	• *Changes in everyday life:* total freedom in the home, but still bound by penance and attempt to improve her image in social environments
	• *Wellbeing:* feelings of guilt and shame overshadow new-found freedom; struggling with her new self-understanding ('I did not do it in order to be mean to him; I just could not cope any longer')
	(The spouse has a stroke and dies shortly after)
	• *New burden:* feelings of guilt due to relief over the death of spouse
	• *Wellbeing:* the burden disappears after a long time, in parallel with a changed narrative:
	• *Active resignation* after a long time:
	1. Acquittal: did not want to hurt him intentionally: I just could not cope any longer; 'No-one is flawless; neither am I'
	2. Paradox: it was a good thing that he died because the alternative would have been worse: he would have suffered more, with dementia and paralysis
	3. After all: still has money, and a caring family
	• *Development:* changed, but more differentiated picture of self: 'No-one is flawless; neither am I'
	• *Change of role:* has become a widow
	• *Change in everyday life:* freedom from the obligations of a housewife

EXAMPLES OF COPING NARRATIVES

You could also present your results as narratives. In the final section about the coping analysis, it is shown how different ways of coping are integrated with different kinds of narratives. Naturally it is relevant to include these narratives in your article, because they illustrate the position of the investigated group in the overall landscape of coping. The coping narratives mentioned earlier are:

- The heroic and/or good luck narrative ('How did I avoid the catastrophe?')
- The narrative of resignation ('How can I go on living with this grief?')
- The narrative of passive resignation or crisis ('Why can nothing be done in this situation?')
- The narrative of extinction of value/goal ('Why this is not worth anything to me – and has never been.')

You may also find new types of narratives among the special groups that you are investigating, which should also be presented as a result. With sex criminals, for example, questions about legitimacy/responsibility are treated through the following narratives:

- *Legitimising, political narratives.* The person is not guilty and is in a certain respect normal, but belongs to a suppressed sexual minority. The question of guilt is simply a question of culture and political attitudes: 'It is the prohibition that is damaging.'
- *Legitimising, innocence narrative.* Nothing happened: 'I only played with the children; they wanted it themselves.'
- *The 'bad' narrative.* 'I am a normal guy who has been bad, but now it is over. I am certainly not a paedophile/ill. But nobody is flawless.'
- *The 'mad' narrative.* It must be a kind of illness; that is the only explanation ('I do not understand myself; I must be ill').
- *'Bad or mad' narrative.* There is no special deviance. Society is full of hypocrites, because many so-called normal men have the same hidden desires for young girls with small breasts (like me).

These narratives reveal the questions these sex criminals are coping with in relation to their position as deviants. The researcher will very likely find narrative patterns in other groups with other kinds of problems offer an insight into typical variations in the group investigated.

CONCLUSION

This analysis, with its overarching concepts, allows the researcher to present a more compact summary of their results in a scientific article. This can be done with the schematic overview, which in its structure is almost the same as the scheme used for the analysis. Furthermore, you may add characteristic narratives, along with the more traditional style of quotation from interviews.

THE METHOD USED ON A REAL CASE

This example of an analysis is from Munk (1999: 291–300). It is given here as a counterpart to the case in Table 31; it is illustrative to see the analysis at work in cases with very different subjects experiencing different burdens. In the case in Table 31 the inner battles of the woman with her self-understanding are the primary issue, and her palliative strategies have become the pattern of her whole life. This also happens with well-functioning people. The emotions of 'guilt' and 'shame' seem to be the fuel behind this intelligent and energetic woman's coping course. She is trapped with a husband suffering from dementia whom she does not love, but whom she cannot leave, according to society's, and her own, moral laws.

Table 32.

A 75-year-old, well-off, married woman, ethnically Danish,
lived together with her husband, who suffered from dementia.
The husband always had OCD. His wife did not love him;
their entire lives together had been as patient and care-giver,
due to his OCD. The wife looked after him by herself.
At the first interview, she has become a widow, and is 79 years old.
She is 80 when she is interviewed for the last time.

	Distressing event(s)	Personal meaning	Emotional implications
T I M E L I N E	**1. Husband's dementia**	1.a Challenge: to live up to the moral imperative to look after one's spouse until they die	1.a Hope
		1.b Loss of personal freedom	1.b Anger/irritation

Coping strategies	Interventions	Outcomes
1.a.1 *Preventative:* increases the care of spouse to full time; considers, but rejects, the idea of getting help in the home, since it means losing control over her home 1.a.1, 1.b.1 *Preventative and palliative:* takes the initiative to transfer spouse to part-time care at the local nursing home; goes away on holiday, but writes postcards to spouse 1.a. 2 *Passive resignation* towards the challenge/dilemma: gives up, by moving spouse to a nursing home as a full-time patient	1. None	
1.b.2 *Restoration of personal freedom* (same as 1.a.2) Gives up trying to be the dutiful wife: takes the initiative to transfer spouse to full-time care at the local nursing home; regains her personal freedom, in fact achieving more freedom than ever before.		Burden 1.b is gone, while abandonment of 1.a (the challenge to care for spouse) creates a new burden (no. 2) *Well-being:* relief and better mood; freedom regained, but not totally *Role changes:* stops being a primary caregiver for spouse *Changes in daily life:* total freedom at home, but bound by penance to spouse and need to improve image as a good wife

	Distressing event(s)	Personal meaning	Emotional implications
T I M E L I N E	**2. Moving husband with dementia to nursing home on own initiative**	2.a Loss of self-image as a dutiful wife	2.a Guilt 2.a Anger at self
		2.b Loss of social image as a dutiful wife	2.b Shame

Coping strategies	Interventions	Outcomes
2.a.1 *Palliative strategies* (guilt): penance towards husband: furnishes a room nicely for him at the nursing home with furniture from their common home and visits him every day bringing cakes to the coffee. Sends postcards when she is on holiday 2.a.2 *Passive resignation* ('self-anger': has spoiled her ideal self-picture and image as the good wife herself)	2.a and 2.b: *Positive intervention:* The leader of the nursing home takes the initiative to tell her that she does not need to come to visit her husband on Saturdays, because he always is absorbed with watching football on TV, and apart from that he is quickly fitting in at the nursing home. This reduces her emotions of anger, guilt and shame	2.a. and b: *The load?* The load does not disappear, but is soothed by the palliative strategies, the support by the leader of the nursing home and her newly freedom *Well-being?* The emotions of guilt and shame are shadowing over the new freedom. Is struggling with a new self-understanding with a starting resignative narrative ('I did not do it in order to be mean to him, I just could not cope any longer) *Changes in daily life:* Chained to a life pattern with penance and attempts to improve her image
		Burden 1.b is gone, while abandonment of 1.a (the challenge to care for spouse) creates a new burden *Well-being:* relief and better mood; freedom regained, but not totally *Role changes:* stops being a primary caregiver for spouse
	2: *Positive intervention:* Husband has a stroke and dies after some days	*Changes in daily life:* total freedom at home, but bound by penance to spouse and need to improve image as a good wife

	Distressing Event(s)	Personal meaning	Emotional implications
T I M E L I N E		2.c *Profit:* greater freedom than ever before	2.c Relief
		2.d Loss of positive self-image	2.d Guilt
	3. Spouse has a stroke and dies after a few days	3.a *Profit:* total freedom from all duties to spouse ('Free at last!')	3.a Relief
		3.b *Threat* to self-image as a decent person ('One should not be made happy by somebody's death')	3.b Guilt

Coping strategies	Interventions	Outcomes
3.b.1 *Passive resignation*		3. The Load disappears
		Development: Changed self-understanding with an active resignative narrative (1. Acquittal: 'nobody is flawless, neither am I. I did not want to hurt him, but could not cope any longer.' 2. Paradox: 'It was a good thing that he died, because if he had survived, he would have had a terrible life' 3. 'After all': 'Fortunately I have nice children and a good economy')
		Well-being: Improves as the formulation of the active resignative narrative is created'
		Role changes: becomes a widow
		Changes in everyday life: Liberated from the life pattern of penance and image improvement
3.b.2 *Active resignation:* (reaches after a long time the ability to formulate a new active resignation narrative which she can live with – this means a new picture of self)		

NOTES

1. Under protest from personality- and psychometric-oriented psychologists (Ben-Porath & Tellegren, 1990; Costa & McCrae, 1990). The whole intention of the theory of Professor Lazarus was to find a different way of understanding stress and coping from the one that prevailed in psychometric assessments (Lazarus, 1991)

2. In an American website that sells the WAYS (http://www.statisticssolutions.com/ways-of-coping-questionnaire-ways/), it is stated that

   The WAYS is excellent for research on coping and scales include: Confrontation Coping, Distancing, Self-Controlling, Seeking Social Support, Accepting Responsibility, Escape-Avoidance, Planful Problem Solving, and Positive Reappraisal. The Ways of Coping Questionnaire:
   - *Identifies the processes people use in coping with stressful situations;*
   - *Can be completed in approximately 10 minutes;*
   - *Can be administered to people of high school age through adult.*

3. 'Stress' is synonymic with 'pressure' and 'weight'.

4. It should be mentioned that the concept of resilience or 'hardiness' has recently become very fashionable, though Kobasa used it as an expression of a personality trait back in 1979. 'Hardiness' is considered a help to the individual experiencing stress.

5. See Holmes & Rahe, 1967. They constructed a ranking list on which life events were normatively considered the worst, the next worst, etc. The death of a spouse is considered worse than divorce. The obvious weakness of this perspective is that such a judgement is dependent on the feelings of the couple. Furthermore, in a divorce the person experiences rejection; when a spouse dies, this is not the case. In other words, it is unwise to be normative about this, and this is exactly what the coping analysis avoids.

6. See Lazarus, 1991.

7. See Bunge, 2006, for a short and systematic overview of different views on the relationship between subject and environment through the history of the social sciences.

8. Scholars do not agree about how the human psyche and personal development over a life course should be understood philosophically, and thus also epistemologically. This is an important point because this manual and its methods take a clear path through this conflict: the transactional point of view.

9. This aspect will be explained in the next chapter on the 'formative elements of the coping process'.

10. The word *mechanism* mostly refers to causal processes outside the human mind. The expression is usually used in the natural sciences. When we are dealing with a person's actions it is a question of *intentionality*. Intentions and causes are profoundly different processes.

11. Again, see Holmes & Rahe, 1967.

12. The only exception is direct physical 'actions' against the body. It does not take an interpreting medium to cause

a bodily reaction of stress, as is seen in relation to surgery, physical violence and very loud sounds. However, stress reactions caused by the person's interpretation of the event may also appear in these situations.

13. The theory, however, is not very explicit about explaining or categorising the environment of the subject. In this respect Lazarus is a typical psychologist.

14. In his last work Lazarus called his later theoretical position 'modified subjectivism'. In this way, he wrapped himself out of the relativism he had been ascribed to due to his earlier works (Bem & deJong, 2004), a position he actually never had. I want here to refer the reader to a former section in this book about the early transactional point of view which he developed in the beginning of his career. Probably underscoring the importance of appraisal and personal meaning contributed to this misunderstanding of Lazarus.

15. Earlier it was underscored that strategies alone cannot explain the outcome of a coping process (Pearlin, 1991).

16. To make sure it should be underscored that the subject itself can be the initiator of aversive courses of events – more or less unconsciously.

17. See i.e. Bunge (2006) for a concise argumentation for a systems' approach. In this reference, it is about understanding of crime and not stress. This is, however, of no significance for the principle.

18. A classic example is the expression 'falling in love'.

19. In this book the concept of resignation is differentiated into three types of resignation: *active, passive* and *adaptive*. The three types all have something to do with a situation in life where your realization of a goal is – or seemed to be – irreversibly blocked in one way or another (*active* and *passive*) or to the source of the situation (*adaptive*). The differentiation is referring to different attitudes to the situation. It will primarily be *active* and *passive* resignation which will be used. It will be explained in the text what they mean. *Adaptive* resignation is referring to conditions in life which are not individual but collective and which you cannot do anything to change or avoid. Typical examples are death and ageing; conditions you have the possibility to slowly adapt to. This very useful differentiation is done by Professor of Psychology Eggert Petersen, Institute of Psychology, Aarhus University, Denmark (1985).

20. In the terminology of Lazarus this is opposed to *problem-focused* coping.

21. This justifies labelling him a neo-Aristotelian, because he builds on an Aristotelian approach to emotions. In his work *Emotion & Adaptation* (1991: 217–219) Lazarus states that Aristotle was the first cognitive theorist of emotions in history because he operated with the same criteria for discrete emotions that he himself uses in his theory of emotions. One of the most well-known philosophical neo-Aristotelians, Martha Nussbaum, also refers to Lazarus in her 2008 book, *Upheavals of Thought: The Intelligence of Emotions*.

22. See Lazarus' discussion of the relationship between cognition and emotion, and the question of causality in relation to the emotions (1999: Chap. 5). Overviews of theories of emotions can be found in Scherer, 2001 and in Solomon, 2004.

23. Lazarus preferred the term 'ego-identity' to 'self', which he saw as referring to what is 'under the skin'

of a person, while 'ego-identity' refers to one's place in the world: 'Erikson's (1950, 1963) concept of ego-identity encompasses the *person-in-the-world*, which includes roles, relationships, and functions in society.' (Lazarus, 1991:101).

24. I let Martha Nussbaum do the talking here because she writes so beautifully about emotions. All emphasis in this quotation is mine.

25. It is in fact a common view in modern psychology.

26. The description may present an ordered, rather slow step by step process, but it may also be rapid, as when an acute danger presents itself.

27. You could say that the concept of coping is in contrast to the concept of crisis, which is limited in time. But they also overlap: a person in crisis is also in a coping situation.

28. In these cases, we often hear numerous excuses and explanations about why things went wrong. Personal ideas about causes or who is to blame are in itself the object of psychological study. In psychoanalysis the term 'defense' is used in these cases. In cognitive psychology the term 'attribution' is used. Always blaming oneself or always blaming others are neither very 'healthy': the first invites depression, while the other entails reduced learning and development. Research on attributions seems to show a certain 'normal' inclination to ascribe the honour of our successes to ourselves and the blame for failures to our environments, while the attributions of other people's successes and failures are quite the opposite (Nielsen, 2005; Larsen, 2009).

29. This case will be used throughout the book because it is so useful in demonstrating aspects of the analysis.

30. If you make your coping categories based on external, visible acts, you will end up with numerous categories. This is quite unanalytic.

31. If the categories are unprecise, that is, overlapping and not fully differentiated, the analysis will become unprecise. This is quite an important point!

32. Earlier in this book I mentioned the phenomenon of 'trio' or 'square' marriages in old age. In such marriages, the dead spouses of the newly married widow and/or widower are still part of the emotional landscape of the new couple, if they were loved when alive. When this is the case the new couple live in a state of 'active resignation'.

33. This will probably mostly be seen in connection with a depression or a shock.

34. This is mentioned earlier in the book.

35. Especially Antonovsky (1985) has introduced the importance of the concept as a crucial perspective on prevention.

36. Today the serious mental illnesses are characterised as perceptual disturbances (Nordentoft, 2009).

37. See WHO's manual of diagnoses, ICD11: Bipolar affective mental illness, p.t. depression, and depressive singular episode with debut before old age.

38. It is important to notice that depression can also develop into a psychosis (ICD11).

39. This is absolutely key to the method in this manual, and must be accepted without question.

40. The only exception here is anxiety, which has no object – in contradiction to fear. This will be explained in Chapter 3.

41. The expressions 'formal' and 'postformal' refer to Piaget's stage theory of cognitive development (Rybash, Hoyer & Roodin, 1986).

42. It should be pointed out, however, that Lazarus warns against considering too deeply the relationship between personality traits and coping, because this can easily lead to an essentialising and primitive categorising of 'how people are'. This entails that the insight into the dynamics and a deeper understanding of, which overlooks what is at stake for the informant. It is important to understand that people with more or less rigid personality traits are nevertheless involved in dynamic transactions and have goals that may be threatened.

43. It was pointed out earlier that in this book 'environment' also means the body, that is, natural bodily processes. From the aspect of resources this also entails the resistance of the body to illness and its potential to self-cure.

44. Folkesundhedsrapporten, Danmark, 2018 (The Report on Public Health in Denmark, 2018).

45. Meaning the ability to anticipate and plan for future eventualities.

46. The French writer Francoise Sagan once said: "Money may not buy happiness, but I'd rather cry in a Jaguar than on a bus." (https://itsamoneything.com/money/francoise-sagan-happiness-cry-jaguar-bus/#.XNHfjC-Q1BI)

47. When the researcher becomes more skilful in the analysis, reading the transcriptions again and again will not take as long. The trained analyser will then be able to fill out the scheme in parallel with reading the interview. The number of times the transcriptions need to be read also depends of course on the complexity of the case in question. It is recommended, however, that you always begin with writing down all the distressing events in chronological order. This is an invaluable help in obtaining an initial overview of the case.

48. Examples: An emotional reaction of *guilt* tells me that I have done or even thought something that conflicts with my ethical norms. An emotional reaction of *envy* towards a colleague who has been promoted tells me that I should have been the one to be promoted, and that my colleague did not deserve it. The colleague has got something that I wanted: a better position and more recognition. This is my reason for not offering my whole-hearted congratulations to her, which leads to emotional reactions of *shame* and *guilt*. This is an embarrassing expression of bad manners (*shame*), and it is immoral not to wish other people well (*guilt*).

49. See, for example, Solomon (ed.), 2004: *Thinking about Feeling: Contemporary Philosophers on Emotions.*

50. For a discussion of the necessary and sufficient conditions for delimiting an emotion, see Lazarus, 1991: 215–296.

51. Especially by the time the brain is fully developed in the middle of the twenties (and not affected by alcohol).

52. In Lazarus (1999: 216–255) *disgust* is excluded, bringing the total to 15. I have not been able to explain this difference. The analysis of emotions has occupied researchers for many years, and will continue to do so; I am sure Lazarus himself would not believe himself to have finished it.

53. This is a fascinating phenomenon which is also seen among parents with handicapped children: guilt can be the only motive in life, and the usual demands to children in order to make them behave in a proper way are completely dismissed because the

guilt overshadows everything and must be mitigated which is not necessarily a benefit for the child.

54. It should be emphasised that the degrading treatment or offence may be caused by the subject themselves, and then the anger is directed at the self.

55. See the European manual of psychiatry, ICD11.

56. Anxiety and fear are expressed in very similar ways; even the language we have for these emotions is not very distinct. The researcher must be aware that when an informant speaks about their anxiety, it might very well be fear. Analytically it is very important to be aware of the difference: the informant knows of the cause of their fear, which is not the case with anxiety.

57. See ICD11.

58. In some cultures suicide due to shame is not considered pathological – in fact, sometimes it is considered 'pathological' *not* to commit suicide in cases of shame.

59. A negative version of this is the husband gives his wife flowers only to be asked the suspicious and angry question: 'What have you done now?' By experience she knows that the flowers are not meant to make her happy, but is a palliative strategy to mitigate the husband's guilt.

60. See ICD11.

61. It is not clear why Lazarus does not consider loneliness to be a discrete emotion belonging to this group. It is very common – at least in Danish – to talk about the *emotion* of loneliness. One explanation could be that 'loneliness' is a composite of other, more precisely definable emotions, for example *grief*. But it is not discussed anywhere in his books, or in Solomon's anthology on emotions (2004).

62. Lazarus connects hope to negative life situations. According to him, hope always arises against a background of a threat or loss. If one is sure that a situation will end well, one feels optimistic, not hopeful (see the discussion in Lazarus, 1991: 282–283).

63. In the case of serious illness, people often seek treatments that are not evidence-based.

64. It is very important to differentiate between the diagnoses of psychopathy and autism: a psychopath is able to 'read' the mental states of other people, but has no emotional attachment. Knowledge about others is used only for the psychopath's purposes. An autistic person – on the contrary – is not able to 'read' others' emotions, and thus sometimes reacts 'empathically' to others' expressed discomfort, mirroring their emotions. A person who suffers from autism is not able to exploit others in a subtle and strategic manner, as is seen in psychopaths (Personal communication: Dr. Bhismadev Chakrabarti, The Autism Research Centre, Dep. of Psychiatry, University of Cambridge).

65. The question of where the initiative comes from is very important for this kind of research, since it helps reveal the resources in the environment of the informant. Only in this way can we obtain a complete picture of how the outcome of the coping course was reached.

66. If the contract is made with a patient, it should be underscored that withdrawal of consent will not have any influence on treatment.

67. The worst-case scenario is that the disagreement between the researcher and the informant ends up in a court case (according to the late Professor Steinar Kvale of the Psychological

Institute at Aarhus University). Professor Kvale always referred to a Norwegian research project which ended in court due to this kind of disagreement (Personal reference).

68. A typical question from an informant is: 'Is this really research?' Some people are surprised that their lives are of any interest for research.

69. Semantic knowledge is stored in concept categories, according to cognitive psychology (Eysenck & Keane, 2005).

70. It is possible to reflect on and talk about these acts, but it is not possible to put all the details of the procedures into words (Eysenck & Keane, 2005).

71. This kind of knowledge 'sits on the spinal cord', because the procedures of practice is 'overlearned'.

72. The way this is formulated makes it sound as if it is a conscious process. It is not. It is possible to decide to remember something special, but in daily life this happens automatically according to certain criteria that are not decided by a conscious process either. It would be impossible to pay attention to every single piece of information we receive in order to decide whether to store it or not.

73. They are both referenced in Thomsen, 2006: 87–88.

REFERENCES

Antonovsky, A. (1985): *Health, stress and coping*. San Francisco: Josey Bass.

Aristoteles (2007): *Etikken*. (Ethics). Det lille Forlag.

Beck, U. (1986): *Risk society - towards a new modernity*. SAGE Publications.

Bem, S. & de Jong, H.L. (2004): *Theoretical Issues in Psychology: An Introduction*. London: Thousand Oakes; New Delhi: SAGE Publications.

Bender, L. (1998): De forrykte gamle – parafreni. (*The daft old people – paraphrenia*). *Gerontologi og Samfund (Gerontology and Society)* 14(3): 62–63.

Ben-Porath, Y. S. & Tellegen, A. (1990): "A Place for Traits in Stress Research", *Psychological Inquiry* 1(1): 14–40.

Berntsen, D. & Thomsen, K.D. (2005): Personal memories for remote historical events: accuracy and clarity of flashbulb memories related to World War II. *Journal of Experimental Psychology General*, May; 134(2), 242-57.

Bronfenbrenner, U. (1979): *The Ecology of Human Development*. London: Harvard University Press.

Bruner, J. (1958): Social Psychology and Perception. In: E.E. Maccoby, T.M. Newcomb & E.L. Hartley (eds): *Readings in Social Psychology*. New York: Holt.

Bunge, M. (2006): A systemic perspective on crime. In: P.-O. Wikström & R.J. Sampson (eds.): *The Explanation of Crime. Context, Mechanisms and Development*. Cambridge University Press.

Carpenter, B.N. (1992): *Personal Coping. Theory, Research and Application*. London: Praeger.

Cohler, B.J. (1982): Personal Narrative and Life Course. *Life-span Development and Behavior* 4: 205–229.

Conway, M.A. & Pleydell-Pearce, C.W. (2000): The Construction of Autobiographical Memories in the Self-Memory System. *Psychological Review* 107(2): 261–288.

Conway, M.A. (2005): Memory and the self. *Journal of Memory and Language* 53: 594–628.

Costa, P.T., Jr, & McCrae, R.R. (1990): Personality: Another 'Hidden Factor' in Stress Research. *Psychological Inquiry* 1(1): 14–40.

Damsholt, T. (2015): Det gode liv i etnologien. (*The good life in ethnology*). *Kulturstudier* 6(1), 37–55.

Deaton, A. (2003): *Health, Income, and Inequality*. NBER Reporter: Research Summary. Spring.

Dilthey, W. (1988 [1923]): *Introduction to the Human Sciences. An Attempt to lay a Foundation for the Study of Society and History*. Detroit: Wayne State University Press.

Draismaa, D. (2006): *Why Life Speeds Up As You Get Older. How Memory Shapes Your Past*. Cambridge: Cambridge University Press.

Due, P., Lynch, J., Holstein, B.E. & Madvig, J. (2003): Socioeconomic heath inequalities among a nationally representative sample of Danish adolescents: the role of different types of social relations. *J. Epidemiol Community Health* 57: 693–698.

Erikson, E.H. (1963): *Childhood and Society.* New York: Norton.

Eysenck, M.W. & Keane, M.T. (2005): *Cognitive Psychology. A Students Handbook.* Psychology Press, Ltd.

Folkesundhedsrapporten Danmark (The Report on Public Health in Denmark) (2018): The University of Southern Denmark.

Folkman, S. & Lazarus, R.S. (1988): *Manual for the Ways of Coping Questionnaire.* Palo Alto: Consulting Psychologists Press.

Gade, A. (1997): *Hjerneprocesser. Kognition og Neurovidenskab* (Brain processes. Cognition and Neuro Science). Copenhagen: Frydenlund.

Haaning, M. (2000): *Familiers omsorg for hjemmeboende ældre demensramte.* (Family Care for Demented Patients Living at Home). Ph.D. dissertation. University of Copenhagen.

Hacking, I. (2010[1990]): *The Taming of Chance.* Cambridge: Cambridge University Press.

Holmes, T.H. & Rahe, R.H. (1967): The Social Readjustment Rating Scales. *Journal of Psychosomatic Reserach* 11(2): 213–218.

Holstein, B.E., Currie, C., Boyce, W., Damsgaard, M.T., Gobina, I., Kökönyei, G., Hetland, J., de Looze, M., Richter, M. & Due, P. (2009): Socioeconomic inequality in multiple health complaints among adolescents: international comparative study in 37 countries. *International Journal of Public Health* September 2009, Volume 54, Supplement 2, 260–270.

Højrup, T. (2002): *Dannelsens Dialektik.* (The Dialectics of Formation). Museum Tusculanums Forlag. Københavns Universitet.

Kobasa, S.C. (1979): Personality and resistance to illness. *American Journal of Community Psychology* 7: 413–423.

Kvale, S. (1989): To Validate Is to Question. In: S. Kvale (ed.): *Issues of Validity in Qualitative Research.* Lund: Studentlitteratur.

Larsen, S.O. (2009): *Psykologiens veje.* (The Roads of Psychology). Systime.

Lazarus, R.S. & Launier, R. (1978): Stress-Related Transaction between Person and Environment. In: L.A. Pervin & M. Lewis (eds): *Perspectives in Interactional Psychology.* Plenum, New York, 287-327.

Lazarus, R.S. & Folkman, S. (1984): *Stress, appraisal and coping.* New York: Springer.

Lazarus, R.S. (1991): *Emotion & Adaptation.* New York: Oxford University Press.

Lazarus, R.S. (1999): *Stress and Emotion. A New Synthesis.* London: Free Association Books.

Loftus, E.F. (2003): Our changeable memories: legal and practical implications. *Nature Reviews; Neuroscience* 4: 231–233.

Loftus, E. F. & Davis, D. (2006): Recovered Memories. *Annual Review of Clinical Psycholology* 2: 469–498.

Loftus, E.F. (2007): Elizabeth F. Loftus. In: G. Lindzey & W.M. Runyan (eds): *A History of Psychology.* In: Autobiography. Vol. 9, Chap. 6.

Luria, A.R. (1983): *Hjernen. En introduktion til neuropsykologien.* (The Brain. An Introduction to Neuropsychology). København: Nyt Nordisk Forlag Arnold Busck.

Lynch, J.W., Smith, G.D., Kaplan, G.A. & House, J.S. (2000): Income Inequality and mortality: importance to health of individual income, psychosocial environment, or material conditions. *British Journal of Medicine* 29 April 320(7243): 1200–1204.

Malmberg, B. (1991): Towards a Coherent Resource Model in Gerontology (unpublished paper).

Mazzoni, G.A.I., Loftus, E.F. & Kirsch, I. (2001): Changing Beliefs About Implausible Autobiographical Events: A Little Plausibility Goes a Long Way. *Journal of Experimental Psychology: Applied* 7: 51–59.

McAdams, D.P. (2001): The Psychology of Life Stories. *Review of General Psychology* 5(2): 100–122.

Miles, M.B. & Huberman, A.M. (1994): *Qualitative Dataanalysis.* Thousand Oaks, CA: Sage.

Munk, K. (1999): *Belastninger i alderdommen.* (Burdens in Old Age). Health, Humanity and Culture. Aarhus University.

Munk, K.(2007): Late-life Depression. Also a Field for Psychotherapists! Part One. *Nordic Psychology* 59 (May): 7–26.

Munk, K.P. (2012): *Coping. Manual til kvalitativ copinganalyse.* (Coping. Manual for qualitative coping analysis). Aarhus Universitetsforlag.

Munk, K.P. (in prep): *Cursed Men and Dangerous Children.*

Møller, J. E., Bengtsen, S.S.E. & Munk, K.P. (eds.) (2015): *Metodefetichisme. Kvalitativ metode på afveje?* (Fetishism of Methods. Qualitative Methods Going Astray?). Aarhus Universitetsforlag.

Nielsen, T. (1995): 'Arbejdsblade' til kursus i fysiologisk psykologi. ('Working papers' for a course in physiological psychology). Institute of Psychology. Aarhus University.

Nielsen, T. (2005): Dagliglivets psykologiske tænkning påvirker unges trivsel. (*The psychological thinking of daily life influences the wellbeing of young people*). *PsykologNyt* 14: 26–27.

Nordentoft, M. (2009): Skal det hedde skizofreni? (Must it be called Schizophrenia?). *Psykiatri-Information* 2: *Psykose.* Psykiatrifonden.

Nussbaum, M.C. (2004): Emotions as Judgements of Value and Importance. In: R.C. Solomon (ed.): *Thinking about Feeling: Contemporary Philosophers Emotions.* Oxford University Press.

Nussbaum, M.C. (2008): *Upheavals of Thought. The Intelligence of Emotions.* Princeton and Oxford: Princeton University Press.

Pearlin, L.L. (1991): The Study of Coping: An Overview. In: J. Eckenrode (ed.): *The Social Context of Coping.* Springer.

Petersen, E. (1985): Træk af resignationens psykologi samt en model af det Danske samfund under krisen ud fra livskvalitetskriterier. (*Trait of the psychology of resignation during the crisis from the perspective of criteria for quality of life*). *Institute of Psychology*, 10(7).

Petersen, J.H., Jeune, B., Kirk, H., Avlund, K., Clark, B., Rasmussen, V.J., Munk, K. & Jæger, B. (2006): *Det aldrende samfund 2030 – Rapport fra styregruppen for det strategiske fremsyn om det aldrende samfund 2030.* (The Ageing Society 2030. Report from the steering group of the strategic foresight on the ageing society 2030). The Danish Strategic Research Council.

Richardson, L. (1990): *Writing Strategies. Reaching Diverse Audiences.* Qualitative Research Methods Series: Vol. 21. London: Sage Publications, Inc.

Robinson, J.A. (1992): First experience memories: contexts and functions in personal histories. In: M.A. Conway, D.C. Rubin, H. Spimler & W. Wagenaar (Eds.): *Theoretical perspectives on autobiographical memory.* Dordrecht, The Netherlands: Kluwer Academic. (pp. 223-239).

Rybash, J.M., Hoyer, W.J. & Roodin, P.A. (1986): *Adult Cognition and Ageing.* Pergamon.

REFERENCES

Sameroff, A.J. (2009): *The Transactional Model of Development: How Children and Contexts Shape each Other.* American Psychological Association.

Scherer, K.R. (2001). Appraisal considered as a process of multi-level sequential checking. In: K.R. Scherer, A. Schorr & T. Johnstone (Eds.): *Appraisal processes in emotion: Theory, Methods, Research* (pp.92–120). New York and Oxford: Oxford University Press.

Solomon, R.C. (ed.) (2004): *Thinking about Feeling: Contemporary Philosophers on Emotions.* Oxford University Press.

Thisted, J. (2018): *Forskningsmetode i Praksis. Projektorienteret Videnskabsteori og forskningsmetodik.* (Research method in Practice. Project-oriented theory of science and research method). København: Munksgaard.

Thomsen, D. (2006): An Interviewer's Guide to Autobiographical Memory. *Newsletter* 1 December, 4: 81–95. Center for Kvalitativ Metodeudvikling, Psykologisk Institut, Aarhus Universitet.

Thomsen, D.K. & Brinkmann, S. (2009): An Interviewer's Guide to Autobiographical Memory: Ways to Elicit Concrete Experiences and to Avoid Pitfalls in Interpreting Them. *Qualitative Research in Psychology* 6(4): 294–312.

Wulff, H., Pedersen, S.A. & Rosenberg, R. (1990): *Medicinsk Filosofi* (Medical Philosophy). København: Munksgaard.